# The
# Shih Tzu

## An Owner's Guide To

## A HAPPY HEALTHY PET

## Howell Book House

Hungry Minds, Inc.
Best-Selling Books • Digital Downloads • e-Books • Answer Networks
e-Newsletters • Branded Web Sites • e-Learning
New York, NY • Cleveland, OH • Indianapolis, IN

**Howell Book House**
Hungry Minds, Inc.
909 Third Avenue
New York, NY 10022
www.hungryminds.com

For general information on Hungry Minds books in the U.S., please call our Consumer Customer Service department at 800-762-2974. In Canada, please call (800) 667-1115. For reseller information, including discounts and premium sales, please call our Reseller Customer Service department at 800-434-3422.

Library of Congress Cataloging-in-Publication Data

White, Jo Ann.
The Shih-tzu Dog: an owner's guide to happy, healthy pet/Jo Ann White.
p.cm.
Includes bibliographical references
ISBN 0-87605-388-6
1. Shih tzu. I. Title.
SF429.S64W48   1995, 2001        95-412724
636.7'6—dc20                     CIP

Manufactured in the United States of America

11   10

Second Edition

Series Director: Kira Sexton
Book Design: Michele Laseau
Cover Design: Michael Freeland
Photography Editor: Richard Fox
Illustration: Jeff Yesh
Photography:
*Front cover photo by Jeannie Harrison/Close Encounters of the Furry Kind*
*Back cover photo by Paulette Braun/Pets by Paulette*
Joan Balzarini: 96
Mary Bloom: 96, 136, 145
Paulette Braun/Pets by Paulette: 12, 43, 47, 83, 96
Buckinghambill American Cocker Spaniels: 148
Phyllis Celmer: 29, 34, 59
Sian Cox: 134
Courtesy of Mike & Lorra Craig: 22
Dr. Ian Dunbar: 98, 101, 103, 111, 116–117, 122, 123, 127
Courtesy of Louis & Wanda Gec: 25
Susan Kilgore: 31
Richard W. Lawall: 5, 7, 9, 18, 30, 32, 45, 46, 51, 53, 55, 57, 60, 61, 62, 66, 68
Dan Lyons: 96
Scott McKiernan: 51, 76, 86
Cathy Merrithew: 129
Courtesy of Sharon A. Milligan: 23
Liz Palika: 133
Jo Ann Regelman: 27
Susan Rezy: 96–97
Judith Strom: 15, 40, 92, 96, 107, 110, 128, 130, 135, 137, 139, 140, 144, 149, 150
Earl Takahashi: 11, 42

# Contents

Welcome
to the
World
of the

# part one

# Shih Tzu

# External Features of the Shih Tzu

Stop

Skull

Muzzle

Crest

Neck

Withers

Back

Shoulder

Stifle or Knee

Hock

Toes

# chapter 1

# What
## Is a
## Shih Tzu?

The Shih Tzu has always been prized as a companion. Because of that, the dog's temperament is of the utmost importance. The Shih Tzu's unique head and expression distinguish the breed from two other related Oriental breeds, the Lhasa Apso and the Pekingese. Although the Shih Tzu is classified by the American Kennel Club as a member

of the Toy Group, the dog is solid and sturdy. Many consider the Shih Tzu to be a "big dog in a little package" in temperament and substance.

In both the pet and show dogs, correct temperament is equally important. Shih Tzu are alert, arrogant and affectionate. They love

5

people and other dogs, big and small. Everyone is this breed's friend. It is most unusual and highly undesirable for a Shih Tzu to be nasty, overly aggressive, nervous or shy.

The Shih Tzu breed standard describes the ideal specimen of the breed. Although the perfect dog has never been born, dog show judging is based on how closely each dog that is entered approaches the ideal picture described in the breed standard. The complete Official Standard of the breed is included for your reference.

# The Shih Tzu Head

Much of the breed standard is devoted to describing the head because this feature most distinguishes the breed. It is sometimes difficult to determine whether head and expression are correct simply by looking at them because skilled groomers can "do up" a topknot to make the head appear correct even when it is not.

## WHAT IS A BREED STANDARD?

A breed standard—a detailed description of an individual breed—is meant to portray the *ideal* specimen of that breed. This includes ideal structure, temperament, gait, type—all aspects of the dog. Because the standard describes an ideal specimen, it isn't based on any particular dog. It is a concept against which judges compare actual dogs and breeders strive to produce dogs. At a dog show, the dog that wins is the one that comes closest, in the judge's opinion, to the standard for its breed. Breed standards are written by the breed parent clubs, the national organizations formed to oversee the well-being of the breed. They are voted on and approved by the members of the parent clubs.

When you think of the correct head and expression, think round, warm and soft. The head itself is large and round when viewed from the front or the side, and the ears are placed so that they appear to blend into the head. The eyes are also large and round, but they should not protrude. Although a small amount of eye white is acceptable, excessive eye white in the corners of the eye or around the entire eye or bulging eyes markedly detract from the desired warm, sweet expression, as does a lack of pigmentation on the nose, lips or eye rims. The eyes should be placed well apart, and the muzzle should be set no lower than the bottom of the eye rims.

The muzzle is short and square and unwrinkled—unlike the longer, narrower muzzle of the Lhasa Apso or the extremely short, wrinkled muzzle of the Pekingese. The muzzle should have good cushioning (fleshy padding), which contributes greatly to the soft expression. The jaw is undershot—that is, the lower jaw is longer than the upper jaw—although the teeth should not show when the mouth is closed, and the lower lip should not protrude when viewed from the side. The muzzle meets the foreskull at a definite angle (stop), giving the desired "pushed-in" look.

*Ch. Heavenly Dynasty's Regal Duke shows off his beautiful head.*

One of the most serious head problems in a Shih Tzu is what breeders often refer to as the "Andy Gump" look. This head is generally oval rather than round and possesses a combination of other faults—a narrow, long muzzle set too low; close-set, small eyes; a lack of stop and of cushioning on the muzzle; and a receding underjaw. Even if the jaw is not actually overshot, the dog looks down-faced and weak-chinned and cannot possibly have the correct expression.

## A Solid, Though Small, Dog

Good Shih Tzu are solid dogs that are surprisingly heavy for their size. Mature Shih Tzu ideally weigh between nine and sixteen pounds and stand no fewer than eight inches and no more than eleven inches tall at the withers. Their length should be slightly longer from withers to base of tail than high at the withers. Most Shih Tzu in today's showrings measure slightly longer than high, although a wealth of hair may make the dogs appear shorter in back than they really are. The chest is broad and deep, there is good spring of rib and the legs are well boned and muscular.

## What's Under All the Hair?

Although a Shih Tzu that is high on leg and narrow in head and body may appear to be in correct proportion due to the wealth of hair, this dog is not. Equally incorrect is the short-legged, barrel-chested Shih Tzu that looks dumpy and squatty. The above two clusters of faults are quite common. Some people are of the impression that a dog that is a only a little bit incorrect in many respects is very close to ideal. In fact, the dog is a poor specimen of the breed and is genetically more likely to produce puppies that are poor specimens than will the dog with only one or two more serious faults. As an analogy, compare the difficulty of replacing your kitchen cabinets with remodeling your entire house!

The body of the Shih Tzu is short-coupled, with little distance between the last rib and the pelvis. There should never be the tuck-up found in breeds such as Afghan Hounds. In a Shih Tzu with the proper spring of rib and depth of chest, the rib cage should drop to just below the elbow. The chest should never be so wide that it forces the elbows out nor so narrow that the dog is slab-sided.

## The Shih Tzu's Build

Structural soundness is as important in the Shih Tzu as it is in any other breed. A Shih Tzu with incorrect structure cannot possibly possess the smooth, flowing, effortless movement called for in the standard. One of the most common problem areas in this breed is poor fronts. The neck should flow smoothly into the shoulders, which should be well angulated and well laid-back and fit smoothly into the body. Excessive development of muscles on the outside of the shoulder blade (loaded shoulders) or shoulders that lack in the desired angulation (straight shoulders) or that protrude from the topline and interrupt the smooth transition from the neck to the shoulders to the withers are undesirable. The shoulder blades should lie flat and toward the spine.

If the front assembly is set too far forward, the weight-bearing muscles and shoulders will not support the head, neck and ribs as they should, and the neck will not blend smoothly into the back. The dog will take short, mincing steps rather than have the correct front reach. When the movement is viewed from the side, the topline will bounce. The stress of inefficient movement will cause the dog to tire easily. The dog will have difficulty holding his head up in the correct arrogant carriage. He may also elbow out, and the pasterns may break down.

The front legs should be straight from the elbows to the pasterns and set well apart to support the broad deep chest. The elbows should be set close to the body, never out or loose, and the feet should point straight ahead. If the front legs are bowed or out at the elbows or the dog is barrel-chested, he will appear to roll like a Pekingese when moving toward you or to swing his legs out to the side and then in rather than extending them straight ahead. This makes for very inefficient and incorrect movement, as does toeing in or out.

*This is a correct Shih Tzu who's been clipped down to make it easy to see build and structure.*

## Correct Movement

Front and rear angulation should be in balance for smooth movement, with good front reach and strong rear drive that are best evaluated by viewing the dog

Welcome to
the World of
the Shih Tzu

from the side. If both front and rear lack the correct angulation, the dog will move with a short, mincing stride, bobbing up and down instead of moving forward effortlessly. If the rear is more angulated than the front, the dog will sometimes move with a hackney gait, picking up his front legs excessively high to keep them out of the way of the oncoming back feet. A dog whose front and rear angulation are not in balance may also crab or sidewind, moving at a slight angle rather than straight forward to avoid having his rear legs interfere with his front ones. In general, a dog whose front and rear angulation are insufficient but in balance will look better when moving than one that has poor angulation in just the front or the rear, but lack of angulation in both front and rear involves two faults rather than just one.

The hind legs, like the front legs, should be well boned, muscular and set well apart in line with the forequarters. The hocks should be short enough to provide sufficient leverage for the desired strong, driving rear movement. Some Shih Tzu have luxating or double-jointed hocks. The tendons that hold the joints in place may be weak, causing them to buckle forward when gentle pressure is applied to the back of the joint. This is incorrect.

## Tops and Tails

When viewed from the side, the Shih Tzu should have a firm, level topline, the head carried well up and the tail curved gently over the back in a "teacup handle." It is extremely important to observe the topline while the dog is in motion because

### THE AMERICAN KENNEL CLUB

Familiarly referred to as "the AKC," the American Kennel Club is a nonprofit organization devoted to the advancement of purebred dogs. The AKC maintains a registry of recognized breeds and adopts and enforces rules for dog events including shows, obedience trials, field trials, hunting tests, lure coursing, herding, earthdog trials, agility and the Canine Good Citizen program. It is a club of clubs, established in 1884 and composed, today, of over 500 autonomous dog clubs throughout the United States. Each club is represented by a delegate; the delegates make up the legislative body of the AKC, voting on rules and electing directors. The American Kennel Club maintains the Stud Book, the record of every dog ever registered with the AKC, and publishes a variety of materials on purebred dogs, including a monthly magazine, books and numerous educational pamphlets. For more information, contact the AKC at the address listed in Chapter 13, "Resources," and look for the names of their publications in Chapter 12, "Recommended Reading."

it is easy to make an incorrect topline appear level when the dog is standing still. Overall balance is of the utmost importance. A too-small head atop a too-long neck is as objectionable as a too-large head atop a too-short neck. A too-long or too-short back, a roach back or high-in-rear topline or an incorrectly set tail also destroys the desired balance. Incorrect tailset ranges from a tail that is too loose (like a Beagle), too tight (curled like a Pug) or too flat (like a Pekingese), to a tail that is set too low at the base of the spine rather than being a continuation of the level topline.

*This seven-month-old puppy already has the long, flowing coat so distinctive of the Shih Tzu.*

## The Shih Tzu's Coat

Another distinctive feature of the breed is the dog's long, flowing double coat, which may be slightly wavy but never curly. The double coat consists of a dense, soft undercoat and a somewhat harder outercoat. A sparse coat or a single coat (one without the desired undercoat) are undesirable. Because the coat is so profuse, it requires a great deal of grooming, although a coat of the correct sturdy texture requires much less care than an extremely soft, cottony coat and is much sought after.

The coat is parted in the center of the back, and the hair on the top of the head is tied into a topknot. The hair between the pads of the feet is cut short, and the feet are trimmed to give them a rounded appearance. Quite often the side coat is trimmed level with the ground, so the dog will not trip over it. The hair around the anus and at the base of the tail and on the bottom of the stomach may also be trimmed for neatness. However, excessive trimming—including the

11

removal of patches of hair around the chest, shoulders or neck with scissors or clippers to improve the outline of the dog—is considered a fault, no matter how skillfully it is done.

## A Rainbow of Shih Tzu

The Shih Tzu comes in a variety of colors and markings, and all colors and markings are equally acceptable. Among the most common are gold and white, red and white, black and white, silver and white, brindle (a mixture of gold or silver and black) and white, solid gold or silver with a black mask and solid black. Less common, but also correct, are liver dogs, which have chocolate brown pigment and brown eyes, and blue dogs, which have gray-blue pigment and blue eyes. These two colors are recessive and are the result of the absence of the color gene for black. Light brown or blue eyes are a fault in any other color. Black tips at the ends of the coat and on the ears and black eye stripes at the outer corners of the eyes on light-colored dogs are common. In a young puppy, it is necessary to look close to the skin to see the color the dog will be when the black tips grow out.

*Shih Tzu come in a wide range of colors.*

It is not unusual for Shih Tzu to change color as they mature. Red may fade to gold and gold to cream. Silver may darken to deep charcoal over time. Some judges unfortunately place undesirable emphasis on flashy markings or colors, but the breed standard clearly states that color and markings are totally irrelevant in terms of quality.

If you have purchased a pet Shih Tzu, chances are the dog possesses one or more faults based on the breed standard that make your pet unsuitable for the showring or for breeding. A thorough knowledge of the breed standard will enable you to understand why you should spay or neuter your pet rather than allow the faults to be reproduced and will help you to recognize a good specimen of the breed. In the meantime, your dog can still be shown in obedience or agility. You might also want to train your dog to be a registered Therapy Dog and allow your pet to bring the same joy to others that he brings to you.

Most breeders are unwilling to sell an excellent show prospect to a home where the dog will not be shown. In many cases, however, the faults your dog has may be obvious only to someone involved in the show world and will go unnoticed by the average person. If you later decide you would like to purchase a show or breeding quality Shih Tzu, you should read every book and watch every video on the breed you can, attend dog shows and talk to reputable breeders. Whether or not your pet is an excellent representative according to the breed standard, the dog can still be an ideal companion and house pet. That is, after all, what Shih Tzu were bred for and why you purchased one. Your pet will—and should—always be "Best in Show" in your eyes!

# Official Standard for the Shih Tzu

**General Appearance**—The Shih Tzu is a sturdy, lively, alert Toy dog with long flowing double coat. Befitting his noble Chinese ancestry as a highly valued, prized companion and palace pet, the Shih Tzu is proud of bearing, has a distinctively arrogant carriage with head well up and tail curved over the back. Although there has always been considerable size variation, the Shih

Tzu must be compact, solid, carrying good weight and substance. Even though a Toy dog, the Shih Tzu must be subject to the same requirements of soundness and structure prescribed for all breeds, and any deviation from the ideal described in the standard should be penalized to the extent of the deviation. Structural faults common to all breeds are as undesirable in the Shih Tzu as in any other breed, regardless of whether or not such faults are specifically mentioned in the standard.

**Size, Proportion, Substance**—*Size*—Ideally, height at withers is 9 to 10½ inches, but no fewer than 8 inches nor more than 11. Ideally, weight of mature dogs, 9 to 16 pounds. *Proportion*—Length between withers and root of tail is slightly longer than height at withers. *The Shih Tzu must never be so high stationed as to appear leggy, nor so low stationed as to appear dumpy or squatty.* *Substance*—Regardless of size, the Shih Tzu is *always* compact, solid and carries good weight and substance.

**Head**—*Head*—Round, broad, wide between eyes, its size *in balance* with the overall size of dog being neither too large nor too small. *Fault:* Narrow head, close-set eyes. *Expression*—Warm, sweet, wide-eyed, friendly and trusting. An overall well-balanced and pleasant expression supercedes the importance of individual parts. *Care should be taken to look and examine well beyond the hair to determine if what is seen is the actual head and expression rather than an image created by grooming technique.* *Eyes*—Large, round, not prominent, placed well apart, looking straight ahead. *Very dark.* Lighter on liver pigmented dogs and blue pigmented dogs. *Fault:* Small, close-set or light eyes; excessive eye white. *Ears*—Large, set slightly below crown of skull, heavily coated. *Skull*—Domed. *Stop*—There is a *definite stop.* *Muzzle*—Square, short, unwrinkled, with good cushioning, set no lower than bottom eye rim; never turned down. Ideally, no longer than 1 inch from tip of nose to stop, although length may vary slightly in relation to overall size of dog. Front of muzzle should be flat; lower lip and chin not protruding and definitely never receding. *Fault:*

Snippiness, lack of definite stop. *Nose*—Nostrils are broad, wide and open. *Pigmentation*—Nose, lips, eye rims are black on all colors, except liver on liver pigmented dogs and blue on blue pigmented dogs. *Fault:* Pink on nose, lips or eye rims. *Bite*—Undershot. Jaw is broad and wide. A missing tooth or slightly misaligned teeth should not be too severely penalized. Teeth and tongue should not show when mouth is closed. *Fault:* Overshot bite.

**Neck, Topline, Body**—*Of utmost importance is an overall well-balanced dog with no exaggerated features.* **Neck**—Well set-on flowing smoothly into shoulders; of sufficient length to permit natural high head carriage and in balance with height and length of dog. *Topline*—Level. *Body*—Short-coupled and sturdy with no waist or tuck-up. The Shih Tzu is slightly longer than tall. *Fault:* Legginess. *Chest*—Broad and deep with good spring-of-rib, however, not barrel-chested. Depth of rib cage should extend to just below elbow. Distance from elbow to withers is a little greater than from elbow to ground. *Croup*—Flat. *Tail*—Set on high, heavily plumed, carried in curve well over back. Too loose, too tight, too flat, or too low set a tail is undesirable and should be penalized to extent of deviation.

*Your pet may not be a perfect specimen, but she'll still be "Best in Show" in your eyes!*

**Forequarters**—*Shoulders*—Well-angulated, well laid-back, well laid-in, fitting smoothly into body. *Legs*—Straight, well-boned, muscular, set well apart and under chest, with elbows set close to body. *Pasterns*—Strong, perpendicular. *Dewclaws*—May be removed. *Feet*—Firm, well padded, point straight ahead.

**Hindquarters**—*Angulation of hindquarters should be in balance with forequarters.* *Legs*—Well-boned, muscular and straight when viewed from rear with well-bent

15

stifles, not close set but in line with forequarters. *Hocks*—Well let down, perpendicular. **Fault:** Hyperextension of hocks. *Dewclaws*—May be removed. *Feet*—Firm, well padded, point straight ahead.

**Coat**—Luxurious, double-coated, dense, long and flowing. Slight wave permissible. Hair on top of head is tied up. **Fault:** Sparse coat, single coat, curly coat. *Trimming*—Feet, bottom of coat and anus may be done for neatness and to facilitate movement. **Fault:** Excessive trimming.

**Color and Markings**—*All* are permissible and to be considered *equally*.

**Gait**—The Shih Tzu moves straight and must be shown at its own natural speed, *neither raced nor strungup,* to evaluate its smooth, flowing, effortless movement with good front reach and equally strong rear drive, level topline, naturally high head carriage and tail carried in gentle curve over back.

**Temperament**—As the sole purpose of the Shih Tzu is that of companion and house pet, it is essential that its temperament be outgoing, happy, affectionate, friendly and trusting toward all.

# chapter 2

# The
# Shih Tzu's
# Ancestry

The Shih Tzu is one of several types of "Lion Dogs" whose ancestors developed in Asia at least as long ago as 1000 B.C. These breeds include the Shih Tzu, Lhasa Apso, Pug and Japanese Chin. The ancestors of the modern Shih Tzu may have been introduced to China from Tibet or Central Asia. Whatever their origin, our  "chrysanthemum-faced" breed had an honored place in the Chinese court, particularly during the time of the Manchu Dynasty (1644–1911).

## Little Lion Dogs

Breeding was done by court eunuchs, and particular colors and patterns of markings were carefully sought and described in flowery prose. A dog with a black body, white belly and white feet, for example, was described as "black clouds over snow," whereas one with a gold coat and a white dome was a "golden basin upholding the moon." The name "Shih Tzu," pronounced "sheed-zoo," actually means "lion" in Chinese. Ancient scrolls showed short-legged dogs trimmed to resemble lions that had heavily bearded and moustached heads quite unlike the smooth-haired head of the Pekingese. The breed's lionlike appearance gave the dog particular symbolic importance.

In Tibetan Buddhism, the lion was Buddha's steed and most important companion and, therefore,

*Typical statuary depicting the little Lion Dogs.*

sacred. Lions were not indigenous to the Far East, however, so lionlike dogs assumed religious significance. Huge stone Lion Dogs guarded many temples and public buildings. Many of these Lion Dogs were in pairs, with the male resting his front foot on a ball and the female resting her foot on a puppy. Often they wore harnesses ornamented with tassles and bells and held ropes or ribbons in their mouths.

Lion Dogs were depicted on scrolls, and lion-dog statues were placed on household altars and ornamented the roof corners of temples, where they were thought to protect the temples from fire. Some of these Lion Dogs are ridden by Siddharta Gautama, the founder of Buddhism, or by the Buddhist bodhisattva Manjusri, from whom the Manchu dynasty took its name. Manjusri was said to have often been accompanied by a pet dog that could be transformed into a lion.

Among its attributes, the Chinese said that the lion dog was to have dragon eyes, a lion head, a bear torso, a frog mouth, palm-leaf fan ears, a feather-duster tail and movement like a goldfish. Lion Dogs (known as Fo or Fu dogs and collected by many Shih Tzu owners) appear not only in Chinese art, but also in the art of Tibet, Japan, Korea, Thailand and Indonesia. Unlike the ferocious lion, the Lion Dogs are often smiling.

Perhaps they reflect the ancient Shih Tzu's arrogant bearing and affectionate personality—or perhaps these attributes were selectively bred for long ago because of the breed's importance as both a religious symbol and a treasured companion.

## Out of the Far East

After the fall of the Manchu Dynasty, Shih Tzu continued to be bred outside the imperial palace by Chinese and foreigners. At this time, the various Tibetan breeds were known collectively as Tibetan or Lhasa Lion Dogs. The first Shih Tzu were taken from China to England, Ireland and Scandinavia in the late 1920s and early 1930s. Without these early exports, we would have no Shih Tzu today. The breed is believed to have become extinct in China after the Communists came to power in 1949 because the Communists considered pet dogs useless consumers of food and viewed them as a symbol of wealth and privilege.

Among the notable early breeders of Shih Tzu in England were (kennel names are in parentheses) Mona Brownrigg (Taishan), Audrey Fowler (Chasmu), Gay Widdrington (Lhakang), Ken and Betty Rawlings (Antarctica), Elfreda Evans

### WHERE DID DOGS COME FROM?

It can be argued that dogs were right there at man's side from the beginning of time. As soon as human beings began to document their existence, the dog was among their drawings and inscriptions. Dogs were not just friends, they served a purpose: There were dogs to hunt birds, pull sleds, herd sheep, burrow after rats—even sit in laps! What your dog was originally bred to do influences the way it behaves. The American Kennel Club recognizes over 140 breeds, and there are hundreds more distinct breeds around the world. To make sense of the breeds, they are grouped according to their size or function. The AKC has seven groups:

1) Sporting, 2) Working,
3) Herding, 4) Hounds,
5) Terriers, 6) Toys,
7) Nonsporting

Can you name a breed from each group? Here's some help: (1) Golden Retriever; (2) Doberman Pinscher; (3) Collie; (4) Beagle; (5) Scottish Terrier; (6) Maltese; and (7) Dalmatian. All modern domestic dogs (Canis familiaris) are related, however different they look, and are all descended from Canis lupus, the gray wolf.

19

(Elfann), Arnold and Jean Leadbetter (Greenmoss) and Olive Newson (Telota). Other well-known early European breeders of Shih Tzu were Denmark's Astrid Jeppesen (Bjorneholms); Sweden's Erna Jungefeldt (Jungfaltets), Anita and Kurt Berggren (Anibes) and Margrete Svendsen (Lyckobringarens); Norway's Ruth Laasko (Zizi); the Netherland's Eta Pauptit (Van De Oranje Manege); and Germany's Erika Geusendam (Tschomo-Lungma). Many of the earliest Shih Tzu in the United States and Canada were imported from these kennels.

*Shih Tzu and their owners at a dog show in England in 1933.*

# Early American Imports

The first Shih Tzu were imported to the United States from England in 1938. Because the American Kennel Club did not yet recognize Shih Tzu as a separate breed, the earliest imports were bred and shown as Lhasa Apsos. The earliest American Shih Tzu descended from the English imports tended to have heavier bones, broader heads, shorter necks and denser coats than those coming down from the early imports from Scandinavia, which tended to have longer, straighter legs, narrower heads, finer bones and silkier coats.

Some of the English-bred dogs had bowed front legs, thought to be the result of a controversial Shih Tzu-Pekingese cross performed by Elfreda Evans in 1952 that was later sanctioned by the English Kennel Club.

Offspring of the Pekingese cross were allowed to be registered in Britain after three generations, but the American Kennel Club required six generations before it would allow Shih Tzu descended from the cross to be considered purebred. This delayed AKC recognition of the breed. Over time, the judicious crossing of the various bloodlines led to the development of a truly American Shih Tzu, combining the best attributes of both types.

In 1955, Shih Tzu were admitted by the AKC to the Miscellaneous Class, where they could compete at AKC-licensed shows. Shih Tzu could not earn conformation championship points, but they could compete for obedience titles. From this time the breed rapidly gained in popularity.

# Formation of the American Shih Tzu Club (ASTC)

The American Shih Tzu Club was formed in 1963 by the merger of the Texas Shih Tzu Society and the Shih Tzu Club of America. A third stud registry was maintained separately by a Mr. Curtis until full breed recognition in 1969. The first Shih Tzu match show in the United States was organized by Swedish-born Ingrid Colwell (Si-Kiang), who did much to promote the popularity of the breed here. Her mother, Ingrid Engstrom (Pukedals), was a well-known Scandinavian Shih Tzu breeder.

Among the other breeders who brought the Shih Tzu to the attention of the U.S. dog fancy and worked for full American Kennel Club (AKC) recognition were The Reverend and Mrs. D. Allan Easton (Chumulari), Yvette Duval (Pako), Margaret and Harry Edel (Mar-Del), Jane Fitts (Encore), Pat Michael (Sangchen), Gene and Molly Dudgeon (Mogene), Jack and Mary Wood (Mariljac), Richard Paisley (Paisley), Bill and Joan Kibler (Taramount), Will Mooney (Bill-Ora), Jay Ammon (Jaisu) and Ann Hickok Warner (Rosemar).

The Shih Tzu was admitted to registration in the American Kennel Club Stud Book on March 16, 1969.

On September 1, 1969, the first day that Shih Tzu could compete for AKC championship points, the Easton's Chumulari Ying-Ying won Best in Show on the East Coast. That same day his sire, the Woods' Int. Ch. Bjorneholm's Pif, won the Toy Group in the Midwest, and Pif's granddaughter Lakoya Princess Tanya Shu (owned by Jean Gadberry) won the Toy Group in Oregon. Twelve days later, Pif became the breed's first American champion. Initially, Shih Tzu in the U.S. showring exhibited great variation in size and type. Over time, they became much more uniform. The present breed standard discussed in Chapter 1 was approved by the AKC on May 1, 1989.

*This is Ch. Stylistic Tiara Preference, ROM, the top winning Shih Tzu in America.*

## Booming in Popularity

By 1969, some three thousand Shih Tzu had been registered by the American Shih Tzu Club. Today the breed has become so popular that about as many Shih Tzu are registered with the American Kennel Club each month as were registered during the thirty-some years prior to AKC recognition. There are many well-known breeders of top producing and top winning Shih Tzu. Recently, the membership of the American Shih Tzu Club voted Ch. Lainee Sigmund Floyd, ROM (Register of Merit), bred and owned by Elaine Meltzer, the most influential stud dog in the history of the breed. Ch. Tu Chu's Mezmerized, ROM, bred and owned by Kathy Kwait, was voted most influential brood bitch. They were considered to have had particularly significant impact on the creation of the more compact and elegant Shih Tzu seen in the showring today.

The ROM title following the names of "Siggie" and "Mez" (and those in the following paragraphs) is awarded by the American Shih Tzu Club to Shih Tzu dogs that have sired six or more American champions and bitches that have produced four or more American champions. Fewer than four hundred Shih Tzu have ever been awarded ROM titles. While winning a ROM is based in part on the number of times an animal was bred and how many of the offspring were placed in show homes, ROM Shih Tzu have generally had a larger-than-average genetic impact on the breed.

*Ch. Snobhill's Free Lance, CD, ROM, is not only the third top winning Shih Tzu of all time, he also earned his obedience title at age seven.*

Ch. Lou Wan Rebel Rouser, ROM, bred and owned by Lou and Wanda Gec, has sired some one hundred-thirty American champions—more than any other Shih Tzu stud dog in the history of the breed. Other influential stud dogs in U.S. breed history include Ena Lane's Ch. Show Off's I've Got Rhythm, ROM; Peggy Hogg's Ch. Dragonfire's Red Raider, ROM; Joan Cowie's Ch. Paisley Ping Pong, ROM; Norman Patton's Ch. Dragonwyck The Great Gatsby, ROM; Joyce DeVoll's Ch. Hodari Lord of the Rings, ROM; Margaret Brown and Luke Ericht's Ch. Shente's Brandy Alexander, ROM; the Eastons' Ch. Chumulari Ying Ying, ROM; and Chuck and Janet Long's Ch. Long's Chiny-Chin Ah-Chop-Chop, ROM. Each has at least thirty champion get (offspring).

Ch. Gunning's Better Half, ROM, bred by Emily Gunning and owned by Dolly Wheeler and Emily Gunning, is the top producing brood bitch in the history of the breed, with fourteen champion offspring. Other top producing bitches include Rosie and Rebecca Cherry's Ch. Ali Aj Wildfire of R and R, ROM; Jim and Gloria Blackburn's Ch. Ming Dynasty's Chinese Sable, ROM; Bill and Dottie Campbell's Ch. Barrington's Windsong of Choo Ling, ROM; Jean Gadberry's Dutch Ch. Indra Shu VDOM, ROM; and Chuck and Janet Long's Ch. Long's Little Lick, ROM.

As of early 1995, based on the total number of Shih Tzu defeated during his show career, the all-time top winning Shih Tzu in the United States was Lorra and Mike Craig and Joanne Rubino's Ch. Stylistic Tiara Preference, ROM.

## Shih Tzu in Obedience and Agility

Although not nearly as many Shih Tzu have earned AKC obedience titles as have earned conformation championships, many dedicated owners enjoy training and showing their Shih Tzu in obedience competition. The first Shih Tzu to earn a CD (Companion Dog title, the first level in obedience competition) was Herb Kellog and Eloise Craig's Ch. Si Kiangs Say It Again, in 1966. The first to earn a CDX (Companion Dog Excellent), in 1972, was Sherry Heldman's Tohatsu of Sherilyn. At only two years of age, Mary Hollingsworth's Omar Playboy became the first Shih Tzu to earn a UD (Utility Degree). Another longtime obedience enthusiast, Pat McCann, had four of her dogs—Pat-Tze Aloha, Pat-Tze Fu Yen, Pat-Tze Chin Pu and Pat-Tze Lu Yence—earn UD titles in both the United States and Canada. A Shih Tzu, Kathy Humphreys Brown's Shasta Marie Tseng Koi, took first place in Novice A at the first-ever AKC agility trial in August 1994—another indication that the breed is as smart as it is beautiful.

FAMOUS
OWNERS OF
SHIH TZU

Zsa Zsa
Gabor

Yul Brynner

Peggy
Guggenheim

Paul Molitor

Elizabeth,
Queen
Consort of
George VI

# A Celebrity Dog of Choice

Some Shih Tzu have become famous because of their owners rather than because of their breeding records or show wins. The British Queen Mother is a longtime Shih Tzu lover. Peggy Guggenheim and actor Yul Brynner were among the many celebrities whose Shih Tzu helped to popularize the breed in the years leading up to full AKC recognition. Most recently, Shih Tzu lover Zsa Zsa Gabor generously donated time and money to Shih Tzu rescue.

*This is the top-producing American Shih Tzu, Ch. Lou Wan Rebel Rouser.*

## Shih Tzu in Other Countries

Shih Tzu were established in Canada by 1935, where they were initially registered and shown as Lhasa Terriers. Although Shih Tzu in Canada are registered in the Nonsporting Group, as they are in Britain, there is very little difference between the Canadian and U.S. breed standards. Many Shih Tzu are shown and win in both countries.

In addition to the United Kingdom, Ireland, Scandinavia, Germany and the Netherlands, European countries where Shih Tzu are popular include France,

Czechoslovakia and Finland. Shih Tzu breeders are also active in Japan, the Philippines, Thailand, Australia, South Africa, Mexico and many Latin American nations, as the popularity of this wonderful breed has spread throughout the world. Some Shih Tzu have also been recently reintroduced into China, although pet dogs are still illegal there.

# chapter 3

# The **World**
## According to the
## **Shih Tzu**

For hundreds of years, Shih Tzu have been bred to serve as human companions, and their temperaments reflect this fact. In pre-revolutionary China, it was a status symbol to own a dog that performed no utilitarian function such as hunting or guarding. The Shih Tzu were highly prized in the imperial court, where they lived lives of luxury.

## All-Around Dogs

Shih Tzu get along well with strangers, children and other dogs, and their small size makes them ideal for today's confined quarters. They are not "yappy" dogs. A Shih Tzu would probably bark if a burglar was picking the lock of your front door. Once the intruder was inside your home, however, your pet would be likely to give the intruder a guided tour! If you want a watchdog, a Shih Tzu is probably not for you. But if you want a small but sturdy, affectionate and appealing companion to share your life, a Shih Tzu fits the bill.

# Hairy Fellows

Shih Tzu are one of the few breeds that have hair (like humans) instead of fur. This means that many people who are allergic to fur are not allergic to Shih Tzu. It also means that Shih Tzu do not shed seasonally. Instead, they shed in small amounts all of the time, just as you do. Much of this dead hair remains on the dog and causes tangling or matting. Because of the dog's profuse coat, the Shih Tzu requires regular grooming. If you are unwilling to either clip the dog down or devote the necessary time to care for the coat, you also would be better off with another breed.

Because of their purpose as companion animals, you will find fewer sex-related temperament differences in Shih Tzu than in many larger breeds. Both males and females are loving and affectionate. Neither sex is aggressive, and Shih Tzu of the same or opposite sex get along well with one another. A male is easier to housebreak outdoors because he likes to mark his territory, but a female is easier to paper train if you prefer not to take your

---

## A DOG'S SENSES

*Sight:* With their eyes located farther apart than ours, dogs can detect movement at a greater distance than we can, but they can't see as well up close. They can also see better in less light, but can't distinguish many colors.

*Sound:* Dogs can hear about four times better than we can, and they can hear high-pitched sounds especially well. Their ancestors, the wolves, howled to let other wolves know where they were; our dogs do the same, but they have a wider range of vocalizations, including barks, whimpers, moans and whines.

*Smell:* A dog's nose is his greatest sensory organ. His sense of smell is so great he can follow a trail that's weeks old, detect odors diluted to one-millionth the concentration we'd need to notice them, even sniff out a person under water!

*Taste:* Dogs have fewer taste buds than we do, so they're likelier to try anything—and usually do, which is why it's especially important for their owners to monitor their food intake. Dogs are omnivores, which means they eat meat as well as vegetable matter like grasses and weeds.

*Touch:* Dogs are social animals and love to be petted, groomed and played with.

pet outside in rain or snow. A male is also easier to keep in coat because hormonal changes associated with female heats can cause a female to "blow" coat seasonally.

## Temperament Differences

Temperament differences in this breed are related more to genetics than to sex. Some bloodlines tend to be "softer" in temperament than others. This trait is wonderful if you want an empathetic snuggle-bunny that will sense your moods and spend hours in your lap having his tummy rubbed.

If you have small children or want a dog you can roughhouse with, a more outgoing Shih Tzu would probably be a better choice. The latter temperament also tends to make a better show dog. You can test your puppy's tempera-

ment to see if he is outgoing or soft. A dominant puppy will be very active and independent. A softer puppy will easily accept handling and be much calmer and more reserved. In either case, the puppy should be curious and affectionate. Either type of temperament can be modified to some extent by the way a Shih Tzu is socialized as a young puppy (see Chapter 4).

*Shih Tzu get along well with everyone, including other dogs. They're also very playful.*

Perhaps because of their long and intimate association with people, Shih Tzu seem almost human. Their faces can be very expressive. At times, when a Shih Tzu is watching people talk, you would swear from his expressions that he understands what is being said. Many a squabble has been prevented by a Shih Tzu pawing in distress at the leg of a person who is raising his or her voice. Shih Tzu often like to watch television—and have definite likes and dislikes while doing so. A few years ago, when Leona Helmsley was much in the news, one of my dogs barked at her every time she was shown in closeup! He clearly did not like the lady, for whatever reason.

## Self-Sufficient and Playful

Shih Tzu are very self-sufficient. If you are busy, they can and do amuse themselves for long periods of time, throwing and catching their own toys, racing around the house like furry dervishes or curling up at your feet simply for the pleasure of being near. Shih Tzu left alone during the day will usually sleep or play with their toys or perch at a window to watch the world go by. They are so easy to live with that many people with one Shih Tzu eventually get another. Breeders frequently joke that Shih Tzu are like potato chips—you can't have just one. Do remember, however, that the fact that Shih Tzu are not demanding dogs does not mean that they thrive in the absence of human companionship. They are definitely "people" dogs.

*Shih Tzu are definitely "people" dogs, thriving on human companionship.*

Even when your Shih Tzu is amusing himself, he will generally do so in ways that get your attention. Your pet might, for example, race back and forth from toy box to living room until every toy rests in a pile at your feet. When one of my Shih Tzu is determined to play catch while we are eating dinner, she bats a ball under the sideboard and begins whimpering pathetically until one of us retrieves it for her. She's learned that we always throw it (to keep her from putting it back under the sideboard). At least that way she gets to chase the ball once, and if she's lucky, we'll continue the game.

At a cocktail party a number of years ago, one of my Shih Tzu felt ignored. She lay on her back in the middle of the floor nonchalantly juggling a toy with all four feet until she became the center of attention. Most Shih Tzu are "toy freaks." One of my Shih Tzu's favorite toys is a large stuffed platypus. She "kills" this toy when she is frustrated, eats her cookies on top of it and sleeps using it as a pillow while holding her favorite yarn ball in her mouth.

*Shih Tzu need regular grooming to keep from looking scraggly and getting matted. This dog is clipped down and has his mustache in rubber bands.*

# Housebreaking Concerns

Housebreaking outside may involve a contest of the wills between you and a dog who prefers to smell the flowers or chase butterflies. Over time, my dogs have come to learn that "Hurry, hurry!" or "Right *now!*" said in a certain tone of voice, followed by lots of praise when they comply, means that outside playtime is over. Inside, it may be more fun to shred the paper than to use it for its intended purpose (fasten the paper down; or cover it with a floor grate from an exercise pen, which has the added bonus of keeping your dog's feet dry). One dog I knew used to compound the shredded paper mess by dumping over her water bowl onto the shredded paper—a great argument for using unprinted newsprint for housebreaking.

When initially confined to a small, puppy-proofed area while being housebroken, don't let your puppy out or give him special attention when he fusses. These responses simply tell your puppy that he will be rewarded for whimpering and barking.

The whole idea is not to give your puppy enough freedom to develop bad habits. One day, after you have praised your pet for eliminating in the proper place for the umpteenth time, a light will dawn, and your puppy will understand what you want him to do. I had one dog that came running out for praise every time he used the paper for his entire life once this lesson was learned.

*Your Shih Tzu can be trained to do almost anything. This one is retrieving over a high jump.*

## Little Chow Hounds

Most Shih Tzu are chow hounds. The cabinet in my kitchen below the counter on which the cookie tin rests needs refinishing after years of having Shih Tzu bounce off it during their enthusiastic acrobatics in response to "Do you want a cookie?" Every dog that ever visited my mother came back overweight because their soulful looks and tuneful yodels (tactics that don't work at home) convinced her that they were starving every time she ventured near the kitchen.

While three or four outings a day, including a brisk walk around the block for exercise, are sufficient for any Shih Tzu, my mother's canine guests also got about six extra walks a day because she would take them out whenever they asked for a breath of fresh air.

Clearly, given an inch, your Shih Tzu will take a mile. This means you need to think about what you do and don't want your dog to do early on. Do you want to allow the dog on the furniture? Will he be allowed to sleep on your bed? Will he be confined (necessary for a puppy) when you are not at home? Clearly, he is not allowed to run out the front door when you open it or leave the backyard or chew the furniture or urinate on the Oriental rug! Once you have determined the limits, be consistent. You will find that Shih Tzu are very anxious to please and that the combination of a single stern correction when caught misbehaving and profuse praise for proper behavior are the best tactics.

## Training Tactics

Sometimes being a bit sneaky is better than provoking a battle of the wills because your Shih Tzu can be stubborn. If the dog removes the *TV Guide* from the coffee table and chews on it every time you go for your morning walk—meaning that you can never catch him in the act—why not just put the magazine in an inaccessible place for a few weeks until he forgets his fascination with that particular object?

Common sense is the real key here. If you get up when your Shih Tzu begins sneezing at you or washing your face at the crack of dawn, your pet will, of course, continue to do so. If he is teething on your antique furniture when you are away, why are you giving him this much freedom when there is no possibility that you will catch him in the act of misbehaving and be able to give him a timely correction?

| CHARACTERISTICS OF A SHIH TZU |
|---|
| Small but sturdy |
| Not yappy |
| Profuse coat (needs regular grooming) |
| Loving and affectionate |
| Can be stubborn |

The "dominant down" used by some obedience trainers to establish that the owner is "top dog" does not work well for most Shih Tzu. You are already much bigger than your Shih Tzu and the source of the companionship and praise he craves. Shih Tzu perform obedience exercises well because they want to please you and because you have made it clear what behavior will elicit your praise or displeasure, not because they have been cowed into submission.

## Take Your Shih Tzu with You!

You will find that your Shih Tzu travels well. If you have to go away and leave him, your Shih Tzu will

*What Shih Tzu excel at are being companions, like this therapy dog dressed up for Halloween sitting with a patient.*

probably pine in a cage in a boarding kennel. If at all possible, see if your breeder will board your dog. If not, try to find a relative, trusted friend or another Shih Tzu owner in your area to care for your pet. He will be happiest in family surroundings while you are away.

The unique charm that characterizes the Shih Tzu makes the dog a delight to live with—and also, as you can see, poses an obstacle to training. Training a Shih Tzu can be both an amusing and a frustrating experience. "Bad dog" generally elicits much tail wagging, many kisses, and lots of "Who, me?" looks of injured innocence. The general response when you try to discipline a Shih Tzu is "How could you possibly be angry with me when I'm *so* charming?"

It's hard to remain stern with a Shih Tzu you've ordered "Down" when the dog enthusiastically flips over onto his back and waves all four feet in the air, wags his entire body and kisses the air. And how can you put up a topknot on a dog who is trying to kiss your nose while you are doing it? You have to steel yourself to avoid succumbing to that charm and letting your dog train you, rather than the other way around. Most breeders know of a home in which the situation escalated until the owners had a chubby, less-than-completely housebroken dog that roused them at five o'clock every morning or that kissed and charmed or pathetically whimpered his way out of being groomed so often that he had to be cut down. Such behavior isn't fair to you or your dog, so be firm when necessary. Rest assured, your Shih Tzu will love you just as much if you teach him to be well behaved.

# More Information on Shih Tzus

## NATIONAL BREED CLUB

American Shih Tzu Club, Inc. (ASTC)
Bonnie Prato, Corresponding Secretary
5252 Shafter Avenue
Oakland, CA 94618
www.shihtzu.org

The ASTC can send you information on all aspects of the breed, including the names and addresses of clubs in your area. Inquire about membership.

## BOOKS

Cunliffe, Juliette. *The Complete Shih Tzu*. North Pomfret, Vermont: Trafalgar Square Publishing, 2000.

Sucher, Jaime J. *Shih Tzu: Complete Owner's Manual*. Hauppauge, New York: Barron's Educational Series, 2000.

## MAGAZINES

*The Shih Tzu Reporter*
(Bi-monthly; strictly Shih Tzus)
1456 14th Street
Los Osos, CA 93402
E-mail: dogmag@fix.net
www.fix.net/~dogmag/shihtzu/shihtzu-home.html

# VIDEOS

*The Shih Tzu in Agility*
Approximately $15

*Shih Tzu Around the World*
Approximately $25

Both videos are available from the ASTC Education Committee. Please make checks payable to:

American Shih Tzu Club, Inc.
5136 36th Street West
Brandenton, FL 34210
www.shihtzu.org/club/astcabout/

*Show Off Your Dog: Grooming Basics*

This Shih Tzu grooming video includes basics applicable to all longhaired breeds. *Show Off Your Dog* features Ena Lane, whose Shih Tzu won Best of Breed at Westminster in 1998. Approximately 60 minutes/ $29.95. Order from:

MJM Enterprises
North Ranch Pavilions Center
1125 North Lindero Canyon Road, Suite A8
Westlake Village, CA 91362
(818) 879-8067
http://members.aol.com/mjmcompany/Basics.htm

# WEB SITES

**Shih Tzu Lover.com**
**www.shihtzulover.com**

This is a great place to start if you're ready to welcome a Shih Tzu into your home. Shih Tzu Lover.com is a Web site created by four breeders. Logon to find out the specifics of each breeder and her kennel's dogs.

**Shih Tzu Rescue Page**
**www.jvars-shihtzu.com/Rescue**

Stop by this Web site for information on adopting a Shih Tzu from a rescue organization. You can also post your own inspirational rescue story online. For more details, send an e-mail to rescue@jvars-shihtzu.com.

**Shih Tzu Net**
**www.shihtzu.net**

Visit Shih Tzu Net for general information on the breed, along with photographs of a variety of happy Shih Tzu. Learn how to groom the Shih Tzu's distinctive "mustache" to keep your dog looking his best.

# Living

with a

# part two

# Shih Tzu

# chapter 4

# Bringing Your
## Shih Tzu
# Home

You should not bring your puppy home until he is at least eight weeks old. The American Shih Tzu Club recommends waiting until a pup is twelve weeks. This way your puppy has had an additional set of innoculations to protect against disease and plenty of time to socialize with his mother and littermates and to begin to be properly taught how to relate to humans and to the outside world.

This socialization process is particularly important if you have young children, who may not understand that rough play can frighten or injure a tiny puppy. (I always tell my grandchildren to sit on the floor to play with a puppy, so they won't accidentally drop or trip over the dog. Children are not very adept at sliding their feet along the ground in the "puppy shuffle.") If you have any questions at any time during your dog's life, don't hesitate to call the breeder. He or she has probably heard your questions many times before and can't help you if you don't ask!

## Preparing for Your Puppy

Before your puppy arrives, make sure you have everything he will need in his new home and have created a secure and safe place where he can spend most of his time until housebroken and used to his new lifestyle. Remember, he is still a baby, and it is your job to safeguard him from harm! I prefer to paper train or housebreak a puppy by creating a puppy-proofed room such as a laundry room or bathroom with a baby gate across the door, so the dog can see out.

## Puppy Proofing

Be sure there are no electrical cords, plants, hazardous household products or other items your puppy might ingest or injure himself with—remember, all puppies love to put anything they can into their mouths. Provide your puppy with toys for this purpose. Shih Tzu of all ages love plush and lambswool and yarn and soft latex squeaky toys. They also enjoy hard rubber chew toys, particularly when they are cutting their teeth. Rawhide is not recommended because it softens and sticks to the moustache when it is chewed and could choke a puppy who eats it.

If your puppy tries to chew on the corners of wooden cabinets or other items you cannot remove from the room, spray them with Bitter Apple or another nontoxic but bitter-tasting substance.

## Your Puppy's Sleep Time and Area

To help your puppy sleep quietly at night, provide a night-light. You may also want to play a radio softly for the first few nights. Do not go to the puppy if she whines and barks when left alone because this will only

**PUPPY ESSENTIALS**

Your new puppy will need:

food bowl

water bowl

collar

leash

I.D. tag

bed

crate

toys

grooming supplies

encourage her to complain more vocally so that you will come back again!

At first, the entire floor of the puppy room should be covered with paper. To avoid inky feet, cover the newspaper with a sheet of unprinted newsprint, available in rolls from your local newspaper or pre-cut from a wholesale paper sup-

plier. Your puppy will generally begin to eliminate in one corner of the room, away from the area where he sleeps and eats. Reduce the paper-covered area gradually to this corner.

Some people prefer to keep a puppy in a large wire exercise pen with a Teflon-coated floor grate rather than puppy proof an entire room. Some of these exercise pens have lids. If yours does, *be sure the lid is securely fastened when the puppy is in the pen.* I know

*While Ch. Xeralane's Unlock the Magic looks pretty posed on this chair, she might make a chew toy out of it if unsupervised.*

of a case in which a puppy jumped up, managed to catch his head between the top and lid of a pen and strangled.

Your new puppy should be given access to other parts of the house only gradually. At first, such outings should take place immediately after your puppy has gone to the bathroom, which he will generally do upon awakening, after meals and before going to bed. Later, as your puppy begins to learn where he is supposed to eliminate and gains greater control over his bladder, the outings can be more extended, but always with supervision.

## Keeping to a Schedule

Until your puppy is totally paper trained or house-broken, adjust your schedule to his. He should spend the night in his room or pen and be put there when you go out or when you cannot keep an eye on him. The whole secret of successful training is to avoid giving your puppy a chance to have accidents on the rug or to chew on the furniture, thereby developing bad habits. Instead, praise him profusely when he uses the paper or eliminates outside or spends the night quietly in his room. By the time he is grown, he will need to be exercised only three times a day. These outings should take place on a regular schedule.

Some people prefer to keep even grown Shih Tzu paper trained. This is an advantage if you don't get home at the regular time one evening, if it is raining or snowing or if your dog has an upset stomach when you are not at home to take him outside.

If you want your puppy to go only outdoors, make the transition by being sure he goes outside often and praising him profusely when he eliminates there. When he uses the papers in the house, don't correct him, but don't praise him either. Eventually, he will stop using the newspapers, and you can remove them.

*Make sure your Shih Tzus' beds have washable covers for flea control.*

Once your puppy has become accustomed to his new home and had his final puppy shots (usually given at sixteen weeks of age), it is time to introduce him to the world. Many people take their puppies to "puppy training classes" or basic obedience classes (often held in local high schools), so the puppies can learn how to behave with other people and other dogs. If you have no children, your puppy can be introduced to youngsters by taking him to the playground or to a local mall. As he is introduced to new dogs and people and objects, be sure that your own attitude is confident, so your puppy will know there is no reason for him to be afraid.

# Socializing Your Puppy

When investigating new situations, your puppy should be praised and rewarded. Trying to force a puppy to approach something that makes him fearful or picking him up and fussing over him when he is nervous generally reinforces fearful behavior. Instead, gently encourage your puppy to investigate. (Food is a wonderful motivator.) If the puppy is still reluctant, try again another day. The games that you play with your new puppy at home will help him trust you and accept you as his leader, giving him confidence when he is in your presence and when he is exposed to new experiences.

Praise your puppy when he comes to you when you call him; teach him to stand for examination (very helpful when visiting the veterinarian); pick him up often; rub his tummy when he is on his back; encourage him to fetch and retrieve his toys and give them to you on command; teach him to allow you to take away his food or move him when he is sleeping; handle his mouth, paws and ears often. Most of all, be consistent, and use love and praise while teaching him that you and other members of the family are the leaders of his pack. Remember, too, that your puppy has a very brief attention span. Corrections are likely to have little impact unless you catch him in the act of misbehaving.

---

## HOUSEHOLD DANGERS

Curious puppies and inquisitive dogs get into trouble not because they are bad, but simply because they want to investigate the world around them. It's our job to protect our dogs from harmful substances, like the following:

### IN THE HOUSE

cleaners, especially pine oil

perfumes, colognes, aftershaves

medications, vitamins

office and craft supplies

electric cords

chicken or turkey bones

chocolate

some house and garden plants, like ivy, oleander and poinsettia

### IN THE GARAGE

antifreeze

garden supplies, like snail and slug bait, pesticides, fertilizers, mouse and rat poisons

# Your Puppy's Crate and Bed

Young puppies need a lot of sleep. They tend to play very hard and then collapse in exhaustion. A toy-sized enclosed crate (which is also approved for airline travel) with a towel in the bottom makes an ideal bed and den for your Shih Tzu puppy. It is small enough for him not to want to soil his sleeping quarters, yet easy to clean if he does have an accident. Later, you can use it when traveling with your pet. If you are using the crate as a bed in a puppy-proofed room or exercise pen, remove the crate door or fasten it open so your puppy is free to go in and out of his den as he pleases.

Once your puppy can sleep through the night without having to elimi-nate, you may want to have him sleep in his crate in the bedroom with the crate door closed. You want the crate to become a safe haven, not a place of punishment. You can initially encourage your puppy to enter the crate with treats and toys; you may even want to give him his meals there.

*Encourage your puppy's interest in the outside world, and praise him when he comes to you when called.*

*Do not* get a dog bed made of wicker or wood because your puppy could chew on it and harm himself. Many older Shih Tzu continue to sleep in their crates. Others like the beanbag beds filled with styrofoam pel-lets or cedar shavings (the latter are said to repel fleas) or the PVC piping and fabric hammock-type beds. Any such bed should have a washable cover for flea control. My dogs, I must confess, sleep on the bed once house-broken.

## Food and Water Bowls

You will also need a metal, weighted plastic or ceramic food bowl heavy enough not to be tipped over and shallow enough for your puppy to easily reach his food. Your breeder will tell you the food your new companion is used to. It is never a good idea to change food abruptly because this can upset a puppy's stomach. Fresh water should be readily available. Many Shih Tzu owners prefer to use one of the water bottles made for rabbits, available in pet stores, rather than a water bowl. This keeps your puppy's face clean and dry and prevents him from taking a bath in his water dish. These bottles can be fastened to an exercise pen, screwed to a kitchen cabinet or placed in a free-standing holder.

## Leash and Collar

Your puppy will also need a leash and collar. Cloth or leather collars do not mat the hair as much as those made of metal. I prefer to use a thin nylon one-piece

show lead with an adjustable neck opening, especially for young puppies. These leads are lightweight and grow with your dog.

If you will be doing obedience training, you will need a round nylon choke collar and a six-foot cloth

*Your puppy will need bowls, food, a water bottle, toys, a collar and leash and other supplies.*

lead. I do not like to let a Shih Tzu wear a collar indoors because it mats the coat. A choke collar could get caught on something, and your puppy could strangle trying to escape if you are not present.

Make lead-training your puppy a game. Let him lead you initially, then gradually train him to follow you, using bait or a toy. If you have a fenced-in yard, get the puppy used to following you without a lead.

## Exercising Your Shih Tzu

A brisk walk around the block will provide sufficient exercise for an adult Shih Tzu. Do not let your dog go outside off lead unless he is in a securely fenced yard, and do not leave him outside for hours unattended. No matter how well trained your Shih Tzu might be, he might decide to wander away, disappear with a stranger, or race across the street after a child or cat and get hit by a car.

Shih Tzu are not basically outdoor dogs and should spend most of their time in the house. They also are not very well suited to walks in the woods because their coats pick up leaves, sticks and burrs. Put your dog in his crate in the car, so he will not be injured if you have an accident. The crate is the doggie equivalent of a seat belt. Remember, if your dog is accustomed to his crate at home, you can take him with you anywhere.

*It's your respon-sibility to keep your Shih Tzu safe and happy.*

# Doggy I.D.

The American Kennel Club requires that breeders permanently identify their dogs, using a tattoo or microchip. Because a tattoo is more easily identifiable than a microchip, I prefer the tattoo. It is also a good idea to tattoo a pet dog because if he wanders away from home, his owner can be located. Attach your dog's rabies tag and registration tag to his collar when you take him outdoors.

# chapter 5

# Feeding
## Your
## Shih Tzu

Very young puppies are fed a special moist diet or soaked kibble until they cut their first teeth (when their teeth come in). By the time you take your pet home, your Shih Tzu should be on a diet based on a quality dry kibble. Young puppies should be fed at least four times a day with a kibble recommended by your breeder for puppies because they are growing rapidly and need extra protein, vitamins and minerals.

Many breeders simply leave dry food and water available at all times or remove food only at night to prevent accidents. Using dry food helps to prevent staining of the facial hair because many canned foods are not only messy, but also contain dyes. Your puppy is your best guide to how much to feed. If she is regularly emptying her dish, you should feed her a bit more. If she always leaves food behind, you are probably feeding too much. Your puppy may go "off her feed" when she is cutting her second teeth because her gums are sore and swollen. This reaction is perfectly normal. Even then, the dry food helps the teething process.

# Understanding Ingredients

Dogs have nutritional requirements that are both unique from ours and from each other's. Pet food manufacturers select ingredients that provide dogs and cats with the energy, protein, and the necessary vitamins and minerals they need, as well as taste and consistency. There are six classes of nutrients that must be fed in appropriate amounts to prevent nutritional upset or deficiency. What they are, what they provide and examples of high- and low-quality ingredients for each are listed below.

**Protein** builds muscles and connective tissue, and influences enzyme and hormone production. Examples of high-quality protein sources are: chicken; poultry by-product meal; turkey by-product meal; meat meal; eggs; liver; fish; fish meal and skim milk. Low quality protein sources include meat, bone or feather meal.

## TYPES OF FOODS/TREATS

There are three types of commercially available dog food—dry, canned and semimoist—and a huge assortment of treats (lucky dogs!) to feed your dog. Which should you choose?

Dry and canned foods contain similar ingredients. The primary difference between them is their moisture content. The moisture is not just water. It's blood and broth, too, the very things that dogs adore. So while canned food is more palatable, dry food is more economical, convenient and effective in controlling tartar buildup. Most owners feed a 25% canned/75% dry diet to give their dogs the benefit of both. Just be sure your dog is getting the nutrition he needs (you and your veterinarian can determine this).

Semimoist foods have the flavor dogs love and the convenience owners want. However, they tend to contain excessive amounts of artificial colors and preservatives.

Dog treats come in every size, shape and flavor imaginable, from organic cookies shaped like postmen to beefy chew sticks. Dogs seem to love them all, so enjoy the variety. Just be sure not to overindulge your dog. Factor treats into her regular meal sizes.

**Carbohydrates** provide starches (excellent sources of energy) and fiber (promotes intestinal health and proper stool formation). Corn, rice, oat meal, oat flour and wheat are all high-quality carbs, whereas soy flour, soybean meal, corn gluten meal and wheat middlings are low quality.

**Fat** stores energy, provides essential fatty acids, and enhances the palatability of food. High-quality fats are poultry, chicken, turkey and pork fat; they are highly digestible. Vegetable oils, lecithin; soy oil; and sesame seed oil are examples of low-quality fats.

**Vitamins** contribute to various functions of the body, from bone development, to sight, to stimulation of the immune system. There are water-soluble and fat-soluble vitamins, and they work alone, together and with other nutrients to do their jobs. Examples are vitamins A, D, C and the B complex vitamins.

**Minerals** are necessary for cellular function and body building—which is using a very few words to cover a multitude of functions. Examples of minerals are iron, calcium, phosphorous and sodium.

**Water** prevents dehydration and is essential to all bodily functions.

Pet food manufacturers are regulated by the AAFCO (American Association of Food Control Officials), which ensures that its products contain the appropriate amount of vitamins and minerals. However, all dogs are different, as are all foods. You can learn more about types of foods and how to read dog-food labels in the sidebars in this chapter.

## Meals and What to Feed

As your puppy matures, you can cut down on the number of meals per day. By six months she should need to be fed only twice a day. Some breeders continue to

---

**TO SUPPLEMENT OR NOT TO SUPPLEMENT?**

If you're feeding your dog a diet that's correct for her developmental stage and she's alert, healthy-looking and neither over- nor underweight, you don't need to add supplements. These include table scraps as well as vitamins and minerals. In fact, a growing puppy is in danger of developing musculoskeletal disorders by oversupplementation. If you have any concerns about the nutritional quality of the food you're feeding, discuss them with your veterinarian.

---

feed two meals a day for life. Others cut back to one meal a day when the dog is a year old. You can change over gradually to an adult kibble when your puppy is a year old. The food should still be high in quality protein. Chicken, lamb or another such ingredient should be listed first on the package, rather than filler. Such quality kibbles are optimally used by the dog, reducing the volume of stool. I prefer foods that do not use ethoxyquin as a preservative because some studies have linked ethoxyquin to immune-system–related disorders.

*Dogs don't get bored eating the same food every day, so don't be tempted to feed table scraps no matter how adorable your dog is.*

In general, adult dogs eat about one cup of kibble per day. Again, if your dog is cleaning up her plate and is thin, increase her food. If she is leaving food behind or is getting fat, decrease the amount you are feeding. To keep your Shih Tzu from becoming a picky eater, leave your dog's meal down for only fifteen minutes or so by about six months of age. If she has not eaten, throw the food away and make her wait until the next mealtime. She will soon learn to eat promptly.

## OBESITY

Obesity is a common problem in mature dogs and can contribute to a variety of illnesses, including cardiovascular disease, pancreatitis, ruptured discs and respiratory problems. Obese dogs are less able to regulate their body temperature and more likely to succumb to heat stress—a problem compounded in Shih Tzu by the profuse coat and short muzzle. You are not doing your dog a favor by overfeeding her!

If your dog has a distended abdomen or fat deposits along her spine and over the base of her tail or if you can't easily feel her ribs through a thin layer of fat, your dog is probably overweight. Your veterinarian can tell you whether or not your dog should go on a diet.

## Supplementing

If you choose to supplement your dog's diet, do so in moderation. A teaspoonful of canned food, meat, cottage cheese or cooked vegetables per feeding to increase palatability is sufficient. If your dog's coat is dry, you may wish to add a fatty acid supplement to her dinner. The only treat your dog should receive apart from her regular meals is an occasional dog biscuit. My dogs also view their daily after-dinner multivitamin tablet, heartworm pill and three or four brewers yeast tablets (said to promote healthy coats and discourage fleas) as treats. (Consult with your veterinarian before supplementing your own dog's diet with excess vitamins.)

### FEEDING SCRAPS

Feeding table scraps encourages begging at the table, contributes to obesity and helps to create picky eaters. Dogs are perfectly happy with the same basic meal every day unless you begin to supplement

---

### HOW TO READ THE DOG FOOD LABEL

With so many choices on the market, how can you be sure you are feeding the right food for your dog? The information is all there on the label—if you know what you're looking for.

Look for the nutritional claim right up top. Is the food "100% nutritionally complete"? If so, it's for nearly all life stages; "growth and maintenance," on the other hand, is for early development; puppy foods are marked as such, as are foods for senior dogs.

Ingredients are listed in descending order by weight. The first three or four ingredients will tell you the bulk of what the food contains. Look for the highest-quality ingredients, like meats and grains, to be among them.

The Guaranteed Analysis tells you what levels of protein, fat, fiber and moisture are in the food, in that order. While these numbers are meaningful, they won't tell you much about the quality of the food. Nutritional value is in the dry matter, not the moisture content.

In many ways, seeing is believing. If your dog has bright eyes, a shiny coat, a good appetite and a good energy level, chances are his diet's fine. Your dog's breeder and your veterinarian are good sources of advice if you're still confused.

with table scraps. At that point, they may hold out and refuse to eat unless you give them a favorite food, feed them by hand or (and I have known several dogs like this) get down on the floor with them and coax them to eat off the floor! Why would you want to encourage your dog to behave this way?

Foods such as very fatty meats and highly spiced foods are almost guaranteed to cause an upset stomach. Others are even more dangerous: Pork and chicken bones can splinter and puncture your dog's intestines; and chocolate, even in small quantities, is poisonous.

## Special Diets

In certain instances, a special diet may be called for. If your dog has diarrhea, your veterinarian may recommend that you give her Kaopectate and feed her cooked ground beef, rice and cottage cheese until she returns to health to rest the intestinal tract. There are special kibbles lower in protein and fat that are recommended for aging dogs.

*All dogs should have—and should be fed—treats. Choose healthy ones, and figure them in to your dog's total diet.*

If your dog has a particular medical problem such as kidney disease, your veterinarian may recommend a prescription dog food designed for animals with such conditions.

If your dog seems to scratch excessively and does not have fleas, you may want to switch to a lamb-and-rice-based kibble. These ingredients tend to provoke food allergies less frequently than other meats and grains and may solve your problem. A middle-aged or older dog that is overfed rich table scraps and does not get enough exercise may develop pancreatitis. In mild cases, the dog may lose her appetite and periodically vomit or have diarrhea. In acute cases, her abdomen becomes rigid and extremely painful.

# All-Important Water

We have already discussed the use of water bottles for your Shih Tzu. Whether or not you choose to use a bottle, fresh water should be available at all times. In general, a healthy, active puppy consumes about one ounce of water per pound of body weight.

If your dog seems to be drinking excessive quantities of water, you may want to have your veterinarian test his kidney function (see Chapter 7). When you travel, it is a good idea to give your dog distilled water to drink because water changes can cause diarrhea. Some breeders recommend adding one capful of raw apple cider vinegar (available in a health food store) to one quart of distilled water to prevent facial staining. The vinegar (which some say is also a natural flea repellant) changes the chemical composition of the tears. Water high in iron can also cause facial staining.

## HOW MANY MEALS A DAY?

Individual dogs vary in how much they should eat to maintain a desired body weight—not too fat, but not too thin. Puppies need several meals a day, while older dogs may need only one. Determine how much food keeps your adult dog looking and feeling her best. Then decide how many meals you want to feed with that amount. Like us, most dogs love to eat, and offering two meals a day is more enjoyable for them. If you're worried about overfeeding, make sure you measure correctly and abstain from adding tidbits to the meals.

Whether you feed one or two meals, only leave your dog's food out for the amount of time it takes her to eat it—10 minutes, for example. Freefeeding (when food is available any time) and leisurely meals encourage picky eating. Don't worry if your dog doesn't finish all her dinner in the allotted time. She'll learn she should.

Bath - 3 weeks

# chapter 6

# Grooming
## Your
## Shih Tzu

Every time a novice owner looks at a beautiful Shih Tzu in the showring with coat dragging on the ground, the first question is "What do I have to do to get such a gorgeous coat on my pet?" To a great extent, a profuse coat is inherited. Even more important, the coat is cared for carefully and regularly, and this care begins when you first bring your puppy home. The real key to a beautiful coat is regular brushing, so large mats never have a chance to form, plus a bath at least once every three weeks. Because a dirty coat mats much more rapidly than a clean one, many show dogs are bathed every week.

# Basic Grooming Supplies

Before you begin, you will need the following supplies, which can be obtained from your local pet shop or a pet-supply catalog.

1. A pin brush with very flexible metal pins for basic grooming and a soft slicker brush.

2. A seven-and-one-half-inch comb (preferably Teflon-coated) with wide and narrow tooth placement for face and feet and for checking for mats after brushing.

3. A comb with rotating teeth or a rake with two rows of teeth set into a wooden handle in a V shape for removing large and stubborn mats. Note that both of these tools remove a lot of hair and are not recommended for show coats.

4. Pint-sized spray bottle (for water mixed with one teaspoon conditioner to mist coat before brushing).

5. Latex bands and colored bows for topknots.

6. Blunt-end scissors (for removing topknot bands and trimming sensitive areas) and straight-bladed seven-to-eight-inch-stainless-steel grooming shears for trimming.

7. Knitting needle or comb with needle (for parts and topknots).

8. Cat or human toenail clippers (for small puppies) and canine nail clippers (for older dogs); styptic powder (to halt bleeding if you cut a nail too short).

9. Ear powder and tweezers or ear hemostat (optional) for removing excess hair from inside the ear canal.

10. A good-quality dryer (preferably a free-standing table or stand model).

11. A high-quality shampoo and conditioner (see comments below under bathing), plus tearless shampoo for the face.

# Basic Grooming

The first thing you must do is to get your new puppy used to being groomed regularly. It is best to begin by brushing your puppy in your lap every day, preferably when he is a bit tired and therefore likely to remain calm. Make grooming a loving time.

Your puppy may initially test you to see if he can convince you to stop. Some puppies shriek and squirm for all the world as if you were committing mayhem. *Do not give in*, but try not to make grooming a battle of the wills because some Shih Tzu can be just as stubborn as you are. Best to use a firm *"No!"* when the puppy misbehaves, followed by lots of soothing and loving and kisses as you proceed.

*When brushing your Shih Tzu, work from the underside up in layers, paying special attention to the armpits and under the ears, which tend to mat first.*

If the puppy learns that good manners will be rewarded and that nothing he does will make you stop before you are ready, the tantrums (if there are any) will eventually cease. If you give in, the tantrums will only get worse, and you will wind up with a puppy that is impossible to groom and eventually becomes so matted he will have to be shaved down. This is unpleasant for both you and your dog, so perservere.

Clean your puppy's face every day and cut his nails and trim the hair between the pads of his feet at least every

*Face - everyday
Nails +
Hair between
pads
2 weeks*

two weeks, so he will have firm footing as his muscles develop. Try to make his first baths pleasurable experiences, so bathing, like grooming, becomes a normal part of his world. Be sure the water is neither too hot nor too cold (test it on your wrist), and try not to frighten him by soaking his face with water.

## Brushing Techniques

As your dog grows more hair, you may want to do your brushing on a grooming table, especially after a bath. Brush gently and carefully in layers, beginning with the feet, legs and belly and working your way up to the center of the back. Because static electricity in a dry coat contributes to breakage, dampen the coat slightly first with the cream rinse and water mix in your spray bottle and brush in long, even strokes. Lift the top of the brush away at the end of each stroke rather than turning it into the coat and flipping the bottom of the brush up, which catches and breaks the ends of the coat. *Be sure to brush all the way down to the skin.*

If you encounter a mat, don't rip at it. Break it apart with your fingers before gently brushing out the dead hair. Large and stubborn mats will be easier to remove if you saturate them with cream rinse and wait a few moments before breaking them up. In extreme cases, the rotating-toothed comb or rake recommended above can be used for dematting. Especially until you become used to the routine, go through the dog with the wide-toothed end of the comb when you are finished brushing to be sure you haven't missed any mats. Check especially in the armpits, on the legs and behind the ears, where the most stubborn and easily missed mats form. Watch for fleas or flea dirt (little black specks), check for ticks and be sure there is no dried fecal matter around the anus.

If you notice any red or irritated spots (hot spots, caused by excessive scratching or chewing), medicate them immediately with antibiotic ointment. How often you will need to brush an adult dog will depend on the texture of his coat. Some Shih Tzu can be done only twice a week; others must be done every day.

# Beyond Brushing

*grab beard to hold head still*

Once you have thoroughly brushed out your dog, use the knitting needle or parting comb to make a part down the center of the back and run the narrow-toothed end of your comb through the whiskers, holding the dog's head still by grasping his beard.

It is much safer to use a comb than a brush around the eyes. If your dog accumulates a lot of matter in the corners of his eyes, you may want to wash his face with a warm, soft cloth or wipe it with a damp cotton ball at this time. Then put up the topknot in a latex band, following the directions in the box on pages 66–67. Clean and check your dog's face every day, even if you do not brush him daily. If you see any signs of eye irritation, contact your veterinarian *immediately*. Neglected eye problems can become very serious quickly.

*These Shih Tzu have been clipped down to make coat care easier on their owners.*

# Topknots

A puppy topknot is generally placed fairly low on the forehead in a single band to catch all the short hairs. Do not pull the hair up too tightly into the band or the dog will rub at it. Later, you will want to do a double topknot to keep the hair from falling forward into the dog's eyes and to hold the topknot more securely.

If you have many short and broken ends on the head, you may want to rub in a drop of Bain de Terre

Recovery Complex (a people-product made by Zotos and available in beauty supply stores) with your finger or brush in a little Shaw's Royal Coatalin (available from wholesale dog-supply catalogs) to prevent further breakage. Dippity Do (a human product) or Sticky Ticky (a canine product) can be used to "cement" loose ends into place when you want the dog to look especially attractive.

*Wrap your dog in a towel to get out excess moisture and to help you cut his nails.*

Many Shih Tzu "change coat" at some point between eight and twelve months of age—that is, they blow their puppy undercoat and acquire their adult one. It seems, during this stage, that the dog mats faster than you can brush, and this is the point at which many pet owners cut their dogs down. Don't despair—just keep brushing. This stage is temporary and usually lasts for about three weeks. Believe it or not, if you've been careful and brushed out the dead hair religiously without badly damaging the outer coat, you will generally find your dog's adult coat easier to care for than his puppy one.

# Bathing

*Never* bathe a matted dog. Brush out the dog thoroughly first. Bathing sets in mats like cement, making them almost impossible to remove. Before bathing, also check your dog's ears and remove excess hair from the inside of the ear canal by pulling it out with your fingers or with tweezers or an ear hemostat; ear powder will make it easier to grip the hair. Such hair prevents proper air circulation in the ear canal and provides a moist breeding ground for infection.

If at all possible, bathe your dog in a laundry tub with a spray attachment. If you use the sink, you will have water all over the kitchen, and using a bathtub is very hard on the back. Be sure to place a rubber mat in the bottom of the tub to give the dog good footing, so he is less likely to struggle. Bathe the head last because this is what Shih Tzu seem to find least pleasant.

Ask your veterinarian to show you how to express the anal glands (when enlarged, they feel like two hard peas on either side of the anus just below the tail). Because the fluid these glands contain is extremely odorous, it should be expressed into a tissue while the dog is in the tub. Place your fingers on either side of the anus and behind the glands and squeeze gently upward and outward to express the fluid.

## Which Shampoos to Use?

Now we get to the much-discussed matter of shampoos and cream rinses. No coat care product is the magic answer for every Shih Tzu coat. Different textured coats require different products, as do different climates and different tap waters.

If at all possible, ask your breeder what products work best in his or her area for dogs with coats similar to your dog's. Nevertheless, you will probably still have to experiment to see what works best on your particular dog. Unless a given product clearly isn't working, use it for a while. If you try something different every week, you will never know what works for your dog. Use recommendations from more experienced people as a guideline, not as gospel; we've all tried and later discarded many products before finding the right one for a particular dog.

Always use a tearless shampoo on the face to avoid irritating the eyes, and try to avoid getting water in the eyes or into the ear canal. Do not use flea control

**GROOMING
TOOLS**

pin brush

slicker brush

flea comb

towel

mat rake

grooming
glove

scissors

nail
clippers

teeth-
cleaning
equipment

shampoo

conditioner

clippers

products on the face. I do not recommend putting pet Shih Tzu down in oil (a procedure used by show-dog owners) because the oil collects dirt, and the coat tends to mat more when the oil is removed. Just leave more cream rinse in the coat after a bath to make grooming easier.

Once your dog is in the tub and wet thoroughly with warm water, shampoo twice. The first one removes the cream rinse and surface dirt, and the second soaping gets the dog really clean. If you have hard water, any shampoo residue (which can cause the dog to scratch) can be removed by pouring a quart of warm water containing a capful of cider vinegar over the dog, then rinsing thoroughly.

Special whitener shampoos may help decrease the staining of white beards (more on this subject appears in Chapter 5). If the staining is due to a bacterial infection, you can use an antibacterial shampoo containing benzoyl peroxide (available from your veterinarian) to kill the bacteria. Be very careful not to get such products into the eyes—a prebath drop of mineral oil in each eye will help to protect them.

In very stubborn cases of infection deep in the hair follicles, your veterinarian may prescribe systemic antibiotics. Do not use bleach on the facial hair if you are not *very* experienced—it dries the beard and causes breakage and could easily injure your dog's eyes.

After rinsing out the soap, put a capful or two of good conditioner into a quart of warm water and pour it over your dog, avoiding the face. Allow the conditioner to remain in the coat for a few minutes, then rinse. I usually leave some conditioner in the coat to help prevent matting, rinsing only until the coat is barely slippery. You can experiment to see how much to rinse out on your own dog for best results.

## Postbath Procedures

Squeeze as much excess moisture as possible out of the coat, and wrap your dog in a couple of thick bath towels. Then hold him in your lap for ten or fifteen minutes, using a corner of one of the towels to wipe the face and blot the ears. You will find that this procedure dramatically reduces the amount of time your dog spends under the dryer.

While your dog is swaddled in towels and more or less captive is a good time to cut toenails. The toenails are also softer and easier to cut when wet. Cut the nails to where they begin to hook over, being careful not to cut into the pink blood vessel (quick) that can easily be seen if your dog has clear nails. If you do accidentally cut too deep and the nail bleeds, use styptic powder to stop the bleeding. Be sure to cut the nails on the dewclaws (the equivalent of your dog's thumb) if he has them. Because these nails do not touch the ground, they will not wear down naturally like the other nails.

## Drying Your Dog

Thoroughly dry your dog with a blow dryer set on warm—*not* hot, which could burn the skin. Test the air from the dryer on your hand to make sure it is a comfortable temperature. Pay special attention to the hair under the ears and on the back of the neck, which seems to take longest to dry.

Brush the dog gently while his coat dries to separate and straighten the hair and speed the drying process. You will find it easiest to use a dryer that leaves both of your hands free to work on the dog—particularly if the dog in question is a squirming puppy.

Once the dog is dry, give your pet a part and put up the topknot. Now is the time to trim the hair between the pads of the feet level with the footpads, so it will not collect dirt, knot and injure the tender skin. The hair on the top of the feet should be rounded, so the dog will not look like it has flippers, and the hair around the anus should be trimmed slightly for neatness. You may also want to trim the hair on the lower belly to keep it from becoming urine-stained and odorous, particularly on a male dog.

If your dog's coat is long enough, comb it down and trim it level with the tabletop all the way around. This will remove split and uneven ends and make the coat look neater and fuller. Do not cut the hair on the muzzle short, even on a pet dog because the short hairs will rub against the eye, possibly causing injury and most certainly increasing the amount of discharge from the eye that probably tempted you to cut it in the first place.

*Trim the hair between the pads of your dog's feet.*

When you have finished, spray lightly with a little of your cream rinse and water mix or a coat-finishing product to keep the hair in place. Then put your Shih Tzu down and watch your pet prance—he enjoys looking good!

## Cutting Your Dog Down

I am notorious for preferring to have my dogs in long coats, although I have been known to cut off the topknots of dogs that look like unmade beds the minute they leave the grooming table once they have finished their show careers. I trim the beard and moustache a little but leave them long enough to give me something to hold onto while grooming and to keep the moustache hair out of the eyes. I cut the topknot hair about one inch long, slightly shorter above and between the eyes.

If you have neither the time nor the inclination to keep up a long coat, it is much better for both you and your dog to keep him in a cute clip than to have you feeling guilty and your dog badly matted, unattractive and uncomfortable. You may want him trimmed short (one to two inches) overall in what is commonly called a puppy clip, leaving only the hair on the ear leathers and tail and the moustache and beard long. Or you may prefer a more sophisticated trim that will make him look a bit like a Cocker Spaniel or a Schnauzer.

You may want to have your dog trimmed by a groomer every six to eight weeks. If you choose to do the job yourself, you will need good electric dog clippers with #10 or #7 blades, scissors and a slicker brush to keep pulling the hair out from the body while scissoring to achieve a smooth effect. When you clip or trim, be sure to begin with a clean, dry coat.

## Choosing a Groomer

While you should always clean your dog's face and keep him mat-free between trips to the groomer, you may choose to have someone else do the really heavy-duty work of bathing, blow drying, nail clipping, ear and anal gland cleaning and, if you wish, haircuts.

You might also have gone away on vacation or had your dog's coat-care regimen neglected for some other reason and find the job of dematting daunting. Large mats *can* be removed with a great deal of time and patience. Try to avoid ripping mats out; the damaged ends will rub against other hairs, weakening them and causing further breakage. You might want to seek out someone experienced in dematting coated breeds to do the job for you, although this is likely to be expensive.

If you are looking for a regular groomer, the best way to find a good one is to ask neighbors, friends, your breeder or another Shih Tzu breeder in your area to recommend someone. Be sure that your groomer enjoys working with animals and carries insurance for accidental injuries and that the grooming area is neat and clean.

Many reputable groomers belong to one or another professional associations. Once you've found a groomer that both you and your dog are happy with, be considerate. Be sure to schedule appointments well in advance and call if you will be late or need to cancel. Tell the groomer exactly what you want done to your pet to avoid unwelcome surprises.

# TYING A TOPKNOT

Once your Shih Tzu has enough hair, it is best to put it up into a double topknot. This kind of topknot gives a more appealing expression, tends to stay in place better and keeps the topknot hair from falling over into the eyes.

Part the hair between the eyes with your parting comb (1).

Take the hair from the outside corners of the eyes (2) and make a straight part just above the eyes across the middle of the foreskull (3).

Put this, the first half of the topknot, into a latex band, then take a few hairs from the back of the banded section and pull them to anchor the back of the front topknot section tightly to the skull. This will "pouf" the front of the topknot, although you may want to use the end of your comb to loosen the front hair even further (4).

Take a semicircle of hair behind the first section of the topknot and band it, again anchoring it to the skull (5) by pulling up on a section of hair, this time in the front of the banded section.

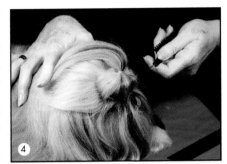

Put a bow on the front section of the topknot, then band both sections together, placing this third band above the band on the front section and below the band on the back section. This will keep the hair in the finished topknot (6) from falling forward.

# chapter 7

# Keeping Your
# Shih Tzu
# Healthy

The Shih Tzu is basic-
ally a healthy dog with
few medical problems.
Many of the health
issues discussed in this
chapter will probably
never be a problem for
you, but they will alert
you to things you
should watch for or
tests you should have
performed if you plan
to breed your dog.

## Finding the Right Veterinarian

When you bring your new puppy home, you will want to immediately take your pet to your veterinarian for a checkup. Most reputable
breeders allow you a day or two to do this and will refund your purchase price or replace your puppy if the dog is not healthy. A health

and vaccination record should have been given to you when you purchased your puppy, indicating whether the dog has been tested for parasites, what innoculations she has had, and what other shots she will require and when.

It is important that you and your puppy establish a relationship with a veterinarian who is knowledgeable and caring. If you do not already have a veterinarian, ask your breeder, other Shih Tzu owners or other dog owners in your town for their recommendations. Because emergencies can happen on weekends or in the middle of the night, be sure that the veterinarian you select is on call twenty-four hours a day or has ties to a twenty-four-hour emergency service.

While many specialized services are available only at large veterinary hospitals, you may prefer the more personalized atmosphere of a small-town veterinarian for routine care. Just be sure you find one who is willing to consult with specialists if a problem that is unfamiliar to the vet is encountered. Choose your puppy's veterinarian as carefully as you would choose your own doctor. You must feel confident and comfortable with whomever you choose. Today's high-tech veterinary care can be very expensive. Health insurance for pets is now available in most of the United States, although coverage is limited and most policies exclude older animals.

> **YOUR PUPPY'S VACCINES**
>
> Vaccines are given to prevent your dog from getting an infectious disease like canine distemper or rabies. Vaccines are the ultimate preventive medicine: they're given before your dog ever gets the disease so as to protect him from the disease. That's why it is necessary for your dog to be vaccinated routinely. Puppy vaccines start at eight weeks of age for the five-in-one DHLPP vaccine and are given every three to four weeks until the puppy is sixteen months old. Your veterinarian will put your puppy on a proper schedule and will remind you when to bring in your dog for shots.

One of the best purchases you can make when you acquire your new puppy is a basic book on veterinary care such as Dr. James DeBitetto's *Puppy Owner's Veterinary Care Book* (Howell Book House, 1995). This practical guide can tell you what to do in an emergency, lists the items that should be included in a

Living with a
Shih Tzu

first-aid kit for your dog and may help you identify any health problems you might encounter, so you can discuss them knowledgeably with your veterinarian. A book, however, is not a substitute for veterinary consultation and care.

## Vaccines

Most puppies receive a series of "puppy shots" against a variety of infectious diseases (distemper, hepatitis, leptospirosis, parainfluenza and parvovirus). **Distemper** is a highly contagious viral disease causing fever, lethargy, coughing, vomiting, diarrhea, seizures and eventually death. **Hepatitis** is a disease of the liver. Its symptoms include fever, abdominal pain, vomiting and diarrhea. **Parainfluenza** is a highly contagious respiratory ailment characterized by a dry, hacking cough. **Leptospirosis**, a bacterial disease carried by many wild animals, causes high fever, jaundice, hemorrhage, bloody stool and prostration. The two leading causes of viral diarrhea are **parvovirus** and **coronavirus**. Both are highly contageous and may lead to death.

Puppy innoculations are generally given at eight, twelve and sixteen weeks (sometimes at six, nine, twelve and sixteen weeks) of age, so your puppy should have had at least one or two innoculations before you brought her home. It is vey important that she receive the rest of the innoculations in the series on schedule to protect her against serious illness. It's also important that she be kept away from other dogs and not be taken to parks, match shows and other places where she might be exposed to these diseases before she has received her final innoculations at sixteen weeks. This schedule is important to adhere to because she has inherited some protection (antibodies) against these diseases from her mother's milk. The innoculations are not effective while these antibodies are still in her system. The age at which these antibodies lose their effect is determined by the amount of maternal protection she originally received.

Thereafter, your Shih Tzu should be innoculated against the above diseases once a year. She should receive her first **rabies** innoculation at six months of age, with boosters as your veterinarian recommends depending on the vaccine used. Rabies is a viral disease that affects the brain; symptoms include extreme aggressiveness or partial or total paralysis. The disease is usually contracted by unvaccinated dogs and cats exposed to the saliva of infected wildlife and can be passed on to humans. It is almost always fatal. Rabies vaccination is therefore extremely important to protect both your dog and the public.

## Internal Parasites

Your puppy's health record will also indicate when your puppy was tested for internal parasites and when and if she was wormed. Thereafter, take a stool sample to your veterinarian when you take your puppy for her annual booster innoculations or if symptoms make you suspect that parasites are present.

### TAPEWORMS

Tapeworms can be detected by finding tapeworm segments around the anus or in the stool. Fresh segments are white and may move; dried ones look like brown grains of rice. It is most likely that you will find the tapeworm segments yourself. Tapeworm can be acquired from uncooked meat or fish, but it is most commonly transmitted by fleas, which serve as an intermediate host after eating tapeworm eggs. If your dog has tapeworm, she may exhibit diarrhea, dry itchy skin or weight loss. She may bite at her rear when a tapeworm segment is emerging. Your veterinarian can provide you with appropriate worm medication, but the infestation is likely to recur unless the flea hosts are eliminated as well.

### ROUNDWORMS

Roundworms, which dogs contract by contact with soil containing the eggs, also are often seen in the stool or may be vomited. They look like strands of spaghetti. Many puppies are born with roundworms because the parasite can encyst in the tissue of the mother and remain dormant until the late stages of pregnancy, when they can be passed along to her puppies. Roundworms are not very serious in adult dogs, but they can make a young puppy severely ill. A puppy with

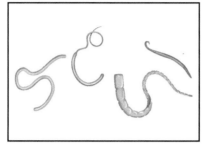

*Common internal parasites (l-r): roundworm, whipworm, tapeworm and hookworm.*

roundworms may have a potbelly and dull coat. She may vomit or have diarrhea and fail to gain weight. Your veterinarian can check for the parasite in your puppy's stool and provide medication to kill the worms. Generally the dog must be wormed twice to eliminate immature roundworms that were not killed by the first dose.

## HOOKWORMS

Hookworms are small and thin. They fasten themselves to the wall of the small intestine and draw blood from their host. The most common signs of hookworm are anemia and diarrhea. The eggs can be picked up from contaminated soil or feces or passed to a puppy by her mother. Your veterinarian can confirm that your puppy has hookworm by the presence of eggs in the stool and provide an appropriate worming preparation.

## WHIPWORMS

Whipworms are threadlike worms that are thicker at one end; they are acquired from contaminated soil. Whipworms may cause diarrhea and weight loss. They are difficult to detect, and it may require several fecal examinations for your veterinarian to identify them and prescribe appropriate treatment. Follow up with several fecal checks to be sure the worms have been eliminated. The same is true for **threadworms**, which cause watery diarrhea and signs of lung infection.

# HEARTWORMS

Transmitted by infected mosquitoes, heartworms are a serious problem in many parts of the country. Adult worms inhabit the lungs and heart and may eventually cause death. An affected dog generally has a soft, deep cough that is exacerbated by exercise. She may appear weak and lose weight. Your veterinarian can confirm the presence of heartworm by finding larvae (microfilarae) in your dog's blood. Treatment is difficult and dangerous. Therefore, if you live in or plan to visit with your dog in an area where heartworm is found, she should be on preventive medication. In warm areas, your dog will constantly be on medication. In colder areas where mosquitoes die out in winter, medication may be needed only from spring until winter.

*Before beginning heartworm medication, your dog must have a blood test to be sure she does not have heartworm.* Only a young puppy that has never been exposed to mosquitoes does not need a blood test first. Otherwise, if your dog has heartworm, the preventive medication could kill her. Heartworm medication is available in daily or monthly doses. I prefer the daily medication because some researchers link the monthly pills to various autoimmune disorders. If you fear you will forget to give the daily medication, however, use the monthly pills.

---

### FIGHTING FLEAS

Remember, the fleas you see on your dog are only part of the problem—the smallest part! To rid your dog and home of fleas, you need to treat your dog *and* your home. Here's how:

• Identify where your pet(s) sleep. These are "hot spots."

• Clean your pets' bedding regularly by vacuuming and washing.

• Spray "hot spots" with a non-toxic, long-lasting flea larvicide.

• Treat outdoor "hot spots" with insecticide.

• Kill eggs on pets with a product containing insect growth regulators (IGRs).

• Kill fleas on pets per your veterinarian's recommendation.

---

## PROTOZOANS

Several common canine diseases, including **coccidiosis**, **trichomoniasis** and **giardiasis**, are caused by one-celled animals called protozoans. The aforesaid diseases can lead to severe diarrhea and are usually caused by poor sanitation. *Toxoplasmosis*, which is most commonly found in cats and can affect humans, can affect the brain, lungs and lymph system. It is detected by blood tests. *Piroplasmosis*, or Canine Babesiosis, is a serious protozoan disease that destroys red blood cells. It is transmitted by the brown dog tick and can be detected and treated by your veterinarian.

# External Parasites and Skin Conditions

### FLEAS

These pests can cause great damage to your dog's skin and coat, so be sure to watch for the fleas themselves, excessive scratching, irritated skin and flea dirt (black specks of flea excrement). If you see any indication of fleas, treat your dog with the products mentioned in

*The flea is a die-hard pest.*

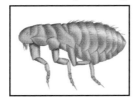

Chapter 6. Severe flea infestation can cause anemia as well as hair loss, particularly in young puppies. In addition, some animals are very allergic to flea saliva.

To get rid of a flea infestation, you must treat the premises as well as the dog. Wash all bedding, vacuum regularly (with a flea collar in the vacuum cleaner bag) and use a fogger containing a growth-inhibiting substance that prevents the development of larvae into adult fleas. Use a fogger in every room of your house in spring and fall if fleas are a problem. This treatment is most effective if you and your animals can leave the premises overnight. You may also want to use a premise spray under tables and other places the fogger might not reach. If you have a cat, put a flea collar on him. Remember that most of the products designed to kill external parasites are very toxic and can accumulate in body tissues. Be sure to carefully follow the directions on the label of any product you use and to watch how you combine them.

TICKS

As you groom, also keep a careful eye out for ticks. If you find a tick, pull it out with tweezers (not your fingers), using gentle and steady pressure. Put antibiotic ointment on the tick bite to keep your dog from scratching at the area. Ticks can transmit **Lyme disease** and other illnesses to your dog, particularly if they are not removed promptly.

If you live in an area where Lyme disease is endemic, you may want to have a licensed pest control

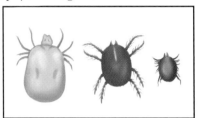

*Three types of ticks (l-r): the wood tick, brown dog tick and deer tick.*

operator spray the perimeter of your property. I use Daminex tubes in wooded areas of my yard; field mice (the intermediate hosts of the deer tick) take the Daminex-saturated cotton balls from the tubes into their nests, where the product kills ticks but not the mice. If your dog becomes lame after being bitten by a tick, she may have contracted Lyme disease. Contact your veterinarian about treatment because untreated Lyme disease causes serious problems.

## Other Itchies

Other causes of itching and skin problems in dogs include **staph** or other bacterial or fungal infections, various forms of **mange** (caused by mites) and **allergies**. Bacterial and fungal infections can be eliminated with special shampoos or medication prescribed by your veterinarian, who can also

*Use tweezers to remove ticks from your dog.*

diagnose mites and provide insecticidal dips to eliminate them.

**Allergies** are often difficult to diagnose. If your dog's skin is irritated at only a certain time of the year, she may be allergic to a specific pollen. Your veterinarian may recommend a brief course of steroids to stop the cycle of itching in a dog with allergies or perhaps a change in diet, grooming products or the environment. In severe cases, you may need to contact a specialist.

*For healthy coat and skin, keep your Shih Tzu well groomed, fed and free from external parasites.*

If your dog's skin is dry and scaly, her coat is coarse and dull, and she has greasy skin, hyperpigmentation and a chronic offensive odor, she may have **hypothyroidism**, an inherited autoimmune disease occasionally found in Shih Tzu and many other breeds. Other signs of hypothyroidism include weight gain, neuromuscular and reproductive problems and blood disorders. Your veterinarian can test for thyroid disfunction and provide medication. A dog that has hypothyroidism and is put on thyroid medication must remain on this medication for life. A thyroid panel and thyroid antibody tests should be done on any Shih Tzu that will be used for breeding.

## Routine Maintenance

**All-over Care**   Many other aspects of routine preventive care such as brushing to check for skin irritation and external parasites; nail and foot trimming; ear and eye cleaning and anal gland extraction should be part of your regular grooming program and are discussed in Chapter 6. During grooming sessions, you can check for the possible presence of other problems such as discharge from the genital region (indicating a possible infection and requiring veterinary attention). Check the anal area to be sure that it has not become blocked by feces. A puppy may have stool catch on the hair around the anus and then sit down, causing such an obstruction.

If you see your puppy **scooting** her rear end along the floor or licking and biting at her rear, such an obstruction is likely to be the cause, although this behavior can also be caused by fleas, tapeworm or impacted anal glands. If the anal area is irritated, apply an antibiotic ointment. Regular grooming will also make your pet better behaved when she visits the veterinarian.

Because you know your pet better than anyone else, you are likely to be the first to notice signs that she may be ill. If she **vomits** or has **diarrhea** just once, do not be too concerned. Dogs tend to eat anything and everything and eliminate what doesn't set right promptly. If she continues this behavior or repeatedly has mild bouts of vomiting or loose stool, particularly if she also appears lethargic, loses her appetite or exhibits other abnormal behavior, consult your veterinarian. Do the same for seizures, recurrent lameness or depression.

**Taking Your Dog's Temperature and Pulse**   When you suspect that your pet is ill, you may want to take her temperature. Use a rectal thermometer coated with a lubricant such as petroleum jelly. Raise your dog's tail and gently insert the bulb of the thermometer one to two inches into her anal canal. Hold the thermometer in place for three minutes. A dog's normal temperature is about 100–102° F.

*To give a pill, open the mouth wide, then drop it in the back of the throat.*

Your dog's pulse, which is normally about seventy to one hundred-thirty beats per minute at rest and faster in puppies, can be taken by pressing the femoral artery located along the inside of her thigh where her back leg joins her body.

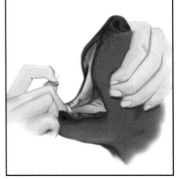

**Giving Medicine**   When you need to administer medication to your dog by mouth, it is easiest to give pills camouflaged in liverwurst or peanut butter. If your dog is refusing to eat or spits out the medication, open her mouth, place the pill on the back of her tongue and hold her mouth closed and stroke her throat until she swallows. If you have to give liquid medication, hold her head up by her chin whiskers and insert the medication in the pocket at the side of her mouth, letting it run through her back teeth and down her throat.

Shih Tzu are difficult to **muzzle** because of their short faces. If this should be necessary, tie a length of soft cloth in a closed loop with a half knot and place it around the nose with the half knot on top of the nose. Make another loop with a half knot and pull it tightly, so the half knot is under the jaw, then tie the ends in a tight bow behind your dog's ears. Do not use a muzzle if your dog is in shock because this may further depress respiration.

## WHEN TO CALL THE VET

In any emergency situation, you should call your veterinarian immediately. You can make the difference in your dog's life by staying as calm as possible when you call and by giving the doctor or the assistant as much information as possible before you leave for the clinic. That way, the vet will be able to take immediate, specific action to remedy your dog's situation.

Emergencies include acute abdominal pain, suspected poisoning, snakebite, burns, frostbite, shock, dehydration, abnormal vomiting or bleeding, and deep wounds. You are the best judge of your dog's health, as you live with and observe him every day. Don't hesitate to call your veterinarian if you suspect trouble.

## Care of the Ears

The Shih Tzu, like other breeds with dropped and hairy ears, is more likely to develop ear problems because the ear gets little air. Cleaning the excess hair out of the ear canal (not the ear flap, where the hairs have nerve endings that make extraction painful) improves air circulation and helps to prevent infection. Some dogs never like having their ears cleaned! If yours is one of these, have someone help you hold your pet.

If your dog keeps shaking her head or scratching at or rubbing her ears or if you notice a foul-smelling or dark discharge when you clean her ears, consult your veterinarian. The problem could be caused by ear mites or a bacterial or fungal infection, and the treatments for each are different. Your veterinarian can test to determine the cause of the problem and provide appropriate medication.

A neglected ear problem can become chronic, so do not wait to see if it goes away by itself. If you have to administer ear drops or ointment, your veterinarian will generally recommend that you clean the ear first with a special solution designed for this purpose, wiping out the excess with a cotton ball. When giving ear medication, put it into the ear and then massage the base of the ear to be sure the medication gets down into the ear canal. Never poke deep into the ear with a swab or other pointed object. This can cause serious injury. Clean only what you can see.

## Care of the Eyes

Because Shih Tzu have large eyes with shallow sockets, their eyes may be more prone to injury than those of some other breeds. If your dog's eyes are red or cloudy or tear excessively, or if your dog keeps squinting and rubbing at her eye, get her to your veterinarian *immediately*. If she has an injury or is developing an infection, prompt treatment can prevent scarring or possibly even the loss of an eye.

Short-faced dogs with shallow eye sockets such as the Shih Tzu are also more prone to **traumatic proptosis,** in which the eye is dislodged from the socket. The eyelids then close behind the eye, cutting off the supply of

*Squeeze eye ointment into the lower lid.*

oxygen to the eye. Proptosis can cause blindness and the loss of the eye if not treated by a veterinarian within twenty minutes. When grooming your dog, be careful not to pull back on the hair on the head and forehead until the eyes bulge.

If you plan to breed your dog, you should have her eyes certified annually by the **Canine Eye Registration Foundation** (CERF; see Chapter 13 for the address) to be sure she does not have any inherited eye problems she might pass along to her offspring. Inexpensive eye clinics are often hosted by various dog clubs; they are frequently listed in the *Gazette*, the magazine of the American Kennel Club (see Chapter 12 for the address).

Among the hereditary eye problems found in Shih Tzu are **juvenile cataracts** and **progressive retinal atrophy** (PRA), both of which lead to blindness. Both diseases are relatively rare in the breed, and a dog with either condition should never be bred.

## CORNEAL ULCERS

These are the most serious eye problem commonly affecting Shih Tzu. An ulcer looks like a small dot on the dark part of the eye; the pupil may appear bluish, and the white of the eye is usually red and inflamed.

A corneal ulcer can be caused by irritation such as that created by abnormally placed eyelashes (distichiasis or ectopic cilia) or by injury (be careful using the comb or brush around the eye). It may also occur spontaneously. An inability of the dog to properly close its eyelid over the cornea (lagophthalmos) or "dry eye," an abnormality of the tear film, can cause chronic ulceration and may require daily eyedrops for the life of your dog.

If your dog has or is developing a corneal ulcer, prompt treatment is essential. An untreated ulcer can cause the cornea to rupture. See your veterinarian at once. Your dog should be given a drop of atropine in the affected eye twice daily, coupled with a drop of Betadyne, which aids in healing. Use an antibiotic that does not contain steroids. Your veterinarian will probably tell you to administer the antibiotic three or four times a day, but every two hours is better if you can.

When administering eyedrops, pull out the lower lid to make a pocket, and drop the medication into this pocket. If the dog continues to rub at its eye, you may need to use a cone-shaped device called anElizabethan collar, which prevents a dog from reaching her body with her mouth or her face with her feet, thus preventing further injury. Once the ulcer has healed over, you will follow up with an antibiotic containing steroids to reduce or eliminate scarring.

# Problems Associated with a Short Face

The short face of the Shih Tzu can contribute to various health problems because its anatomical conformation compresses the nasal cavity, pharynx, larynx and surrounding tissues into a small space. Shih Tzu puppies may snore, snort, bubble or sniffle, particularly while teething. These symptoms are no cause for concern if the nasal discharge is clear and the dog is thriving.

**Slightly pinched nostrils** are very common in this breed and normally correct themselves as the dog matures. If your dog's nostrils are extremely pinched, so she can only breathe through her mouth and has trouble eating, even after she has cut her adult teeth, you may wish to have her examined by a specialist.

Severe snorting respiration and difficulty in breathing may, in rare cases, lead to cyanosis and collapse due to obstructive respiratory disease caused by stenotic nares, elongated soft palates and eversion of the lateral ventricles. In such extreme cases, corrective surgery may be necessary to open the airway. Many veterinarians unfamiliar with the breed, however, are much too quick to recommend such surgery. If your dog is thriving or in the teething stage, just give the symptoms a little time.

Even with an adult, it is important to be sure that your short-faced Shih Tzu does not become overheated. Do not leave her in a car with the windows closed or take her for long walks outdoors when the weather is hot.

Blue ice packs will help keep your dog cool when you travel in the "dog days" of summer.

# Care of the Teeth and Gums

The Shih Tzu's undershot bite frequently causes her to lose some of her front teeth at an early age. Missing or

*Check your dog's teeth frequently and brush them regularly.*

misaligned teeth or retained baby teeth are quite common in the breed.

Your Shih Tzu will begin to acquire her permanent teeth at about four or five months of age. At this time her gums may become swollen and sore, and she may go off her feed. Dog biscuits and hard chew toys help the permanent teeth to emerge. If you notice a retained baby tooth, wiggle it with your fingernail to help it come out. Retained baby teeth can cause the permanent teeth to be pushed out of alignment.

To prevent **tooth decay** and **gum disease,** give your dog kibble, dog biscuits and hard toys to chew on and have your veterinarian show you how to clean your dog's teeth. If tartar and plaque build up, you may have to have your veterinarian scale your dog's teeth under anesthesia, so it is best to make dental care part of your regular routine. Neglected teeth and gums can lead to infection and cause serious health problems for your dog later in life.

# Inherited Disorders

A number of genetic disorders can be found in Shih Tzu in addition to the hypothyroidism and eye problems discussed earlier.

**Renal dysplasia,** a developmental defect of the kidneys, is the most serious inherited disorder found in Shih Tzu. It is also present in Lhasa Apsos and, less frequently, in some other breeds. In renal dysplasia, a varying number of nephrons (urine-forming units) in the kidneys never mature and some may be replaced with fibrous tissue. Other signs of the disease include diffuse interstitial fibrosis in the cortex and medula, dilated and hypoplastic tubles and glomeruli in reduced numbers and varying sizes.

Severely affected puppies, with more than thirty-five percent hypoplastic glomeruli, drink and urinate excessively and are smaller than normal (generally less than three pounds at five months of age). Rather quickly they begin to vomit, become weak, debilitated and dehydrated and ultimately die of kidney failure. Moderately affected puppies may appear normal until five or six months of age and then follow the same course.

Although the only definitive test for the disease now (and the only test that will detect mildly affected dogs) is a wide wedge kidney biopsy, the presence of renal dysplasia can be suspected in young animals having elevated BUN and creatinine blood tests and extremely dilute urine as measured by a urine-specific gravity test.

Moderately affected puppies showing no clinical signs of the disease may be suspected if an ultrasound examination shows smaller than normal size kidneys that may be scarred or irregular in shape with defects in the collecting ducts in the renal pelvis.

*Because of their facial structure, Shih Tzu are prone to eye problems. Check the eyes regularly.*

It is unwise to biopsy animals with poor results on these tests because they are a surgical risk. Instead, your veterinarian can recommend a special diet to help alleviate the symptoms of the disease.

A wedge biopsy is recommended for all breeding stock, particularly any animal that might have produced affected puppies; a needle biopsy does not provide enough tissue for examination and is of little value.

The tissue can be collected by your veterinarian but should be sent to an experienced pathologist familiar with this disease for examination.

At the least, an ultrasound examination of the kidneys should be performed on all breeding stock because it can detect many moderate carriers. The urine and blood tests remain normal until more than seventy percent of the kidney is destroyed, and these tests may also be abnormal due to other kidney diseases, so they are of no value in detecting moderately and slightly affected dogs.

Only a small percentage of Shih Tzu are severely affected by renal dysplasia and will die of renal failure. The mode of inheritance of this disease is unclear, partly because slightly affected dogs can live a normal life with normal renal function while still passing along some degree of the defect to their offspring.

*An Elizabethan collar keeps your dog from licking a fresh wound.*

To gain more knowledge about the disease and the way in which it is inherited, the American Shih Tzu Club recommends that wedge biopsy tissue and the kidneys from Shih Tzu over eight weeks of age that die from any cause be sent, along with a pedigree, to Dr. Kenneth C. Bovee, University of Pennsylvania School of Veterinary Medicine, Department of Clinical Studies, 3850 Spruce Street, Philadelphia, PA 19104–6010. Your veterinarian can call Dr. Bovee at (215) 898-4454 to discuss how the kidney tissue should be collected and preserved.

Symptoms such as those just described in an elderly dog may be a sign of various "old age" kidney diseases found in all breeds of dogs. Again, your veterinarian will want to perform blood and urine tests and perhaps prescribe a special diet. These diseases can also obscure the presence of renal dysplasia in the tissue of elderly animals.

## STONES

Shih Tzu may be affected with **kidney or bladder stones**. Symptoms of bladder stones include urinary blockage, painful voiding, blood in the urine and cystitis. Large stones are generally removed surgically. Smaller stones can be dissolved and new stones kept from forming with a special diet prescribed by your veterinarian. Infections and other types of obstructions may cause similar symptoms, all of which should be treated promptly by your veterinarian.

## PORTAL SYSTEMIC SHUNT

This is another inherited disease that may be found, in rare instances, in Shih Tzu and several other smaller breeds. In this liver shunt disease, blood is diverted around the liver into the bloodstream without being detoxified. Many cases are diagnosed in young animals. Those affected are depressed, thin and have trouble gaining weight. They may periodically exhibit peculiar behavior such as bouts of aggression, staggering, pacing, circling, head pressing, blindness, deafness, tremors and seizures. Your veterinarian can test for the presence of the disease and provide a special diet. The defect can be surgically corrected; without surgery, severely affected animals probably will die of liver failure.

---

### A FIRST-AID KIT

Keep a canine first-aid kit on hand for general care and emergencies. Check it periodically to make sure liquids haven't spilled or dried up, and replace medications and materials after they're used. Your kit should include:

Activated charcoal tablets

Adhesive tape
(1 and 2 inches wide)

Antibacterial ointment
(for skin and eyes)

Aspirin (buffered or enteric coated, *not* Ibuprofen)

Bandages: Gauze rolls (1 and 2 inches wide) and dressing pads

Cotton balls

Diarrhea medicine

Dosing syringe

Hydrogen peroxide (3%)

Petroleum jelly

Rectal thermometer

Rubber gloves

Rubbing alcohol

Scissors

Tourniquet

Towel

Tweezers

# HERNIAS

Small **umbilical hernias** are frequently found in Shih Tzu puppies. These may be inherited or may be due to tension on the umbilical cord at birth. These hernias unless they are very large usually close by themselves, so do not be too quick to perform corrective surgery. **Inguinal hernias**, found in the groin area, are much more serious. Many will require surgical correction, and dogs with inguinal hernias should not be bred.

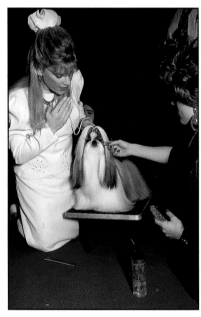

*Responsible owners know that only the very best Shih Tzu should be bred. These owners have a beautiful Shih Tzu, but they know health and temperament are equally important traits to pass on.*

# IMMUNE-SYSTEM DISORDERS

Shih Tzu are, like many breeds of dogs, affected by various disorders of the immune system. **Hypothyroidism** is perhaps the most common. It is a deficiency in the production of the hormones from the thyroid gland. Such a deficiency causes hair to become brittle and fall out easily. The dog's skin will also get thick and turn a darker color. Thyroid also controls metabolism, and a dog with hypothyroidism will be lethargic, tend to be fat and will have limited energy. The deficiency can range from mild to severe; mild cases may not even appear to be present, though a blood test can determine it.

Another immune-system disorder is **von Willebrand's disease** (vWD), a blood-clotting disorder. Testing for this disorder is strongly recommended because a dog with severe von Willebrand's disease could bleed to death during routine surgery. Your veterinarian can draw the blood for this test, but it must be drawn and shipped in a very specific manner and sent to the Veterinary Hematology Laboratory of the New York State Department of Health, Wadsworth Center for Labs and Research, Albany, NY 12201, for a reading.

Contact them first for vials and instructions. In the absence of such a test, have your vet do a "toenail bleeding test" before surgery to be sure your dog's blood is clotting normally.

Other disorders of the immune system include various forms of blood cancer and **autoimmune hemolytic anemia**, in which the dog destroys its own red blood cells.

## BONE AND JOINT DISORDERS

Like other breeds, Shih Tzu may inherit **hip dysplasia** and other bone and joint disorders such as spinal disk problems, slipping kneecaps, popping hocks and elbow dysplasia. Although such diseases in small breeds generally tend not to be crippling, they can be very painful. If you plan to breed your dog, first have it certified by the Orthopedic Foundation for Animals (OFA; see Chapter 13). Lameness in elderly dogs may be caused by arthritis. Your veterinarian will recommend aspirin to relieve the pain of arthritis and moderate exercise to prevent joint stiffness.

## HEART DISEASE

Heart disease can be both inherited and acquired. When your dog visits your veterinarian for his annual physical, his heart will be checked for signs of abnormality. Some of the symptoms of heart disease include labored breathing, coughing or wheezing, weakness, loss of appetite and a watery swelling of the abdomen (edema). Surgery or therapy can cure some cardiac problems or greatly extend the life of an affected pet.

### ADVANTAGES OF SPAY/NEUTER

The greatest advantage of spaying (for females) or neutering (for males) your dog is that you are guaranteed your dog will not produce puppies. There are too many puppies already available for too few homes. There are other advantages as well.

#### ADVANTAGES OF SPAYING

No messy heats.

No "suitors" howling at your windows or waiting in your yard.

Decreased incidences of pyometra (disease of the uterus) and breast cancer.

#### ADVANTAGES OF NEUTERING

Lessens male aggressive and territorial behaviors, but doesn't affect the dog's personality. Behaviors are often owner-induced, so neutering is not the only answer, but it is a good start.

Prevents the need to roam in search of bitches in season.

Decreased incidences of urogenital diseases.

# Spaying and Neutering: Why It's Best not to Breed

The earlier discussion of the inherited diseases should indicate one of the reasons why only knowledgeable individuals should breed dogs. No one wants to produce unhealthy animals that will die in the nest or cause heartbreak to their owners.

Because your dog is registered with the American Kennel Club does not mean that your is a quality representative of the breed; it only means that both parents were registered with the AKC. Most purebred dogs should not be bred, and many responsible breeders sell pet dogs on spay and neuter contracts (withholding papers until the surgery is performed) or with AKC limited registration, under which their offspring cannot be registered as purebred.

*Run your hands regularly over your dog to feel for any injuries.*

Breeding should be done only for the goals of improving the breed's health, conformation and temperament. It requires a great deal of knowledge and study.

If you own a male, people are not likely to be beating down your door to use him to stud unless he demonstrates his quality in the showring and has a distinguished pedigree. Moreover, once bred, he may begin lifting his leg on your furniture and riding your guests.

If you own a female, whelping a litter can be a joy—or a tragedy. You could wind up losing both puppies and mother, and you are unlikely to make any money after paying for health care, stud fees, food and advertising the litter. If you want another dog that looks just like your darling, the best way to get one is to go out and buy another Shih Tzu! Leave the responsibility and possible pain of breeding to someone more knowledgeable.

First-time breeders also generally do not have the contacts to sell their puppies—buyers tend to evaporate at the time of sale. Raising a litter successfully takes a lot of time and expertise. Most important, *what will happen to the puppies you have brought into the world?* You may think they have found good homes, but even if they have, what happens if their owners move or divorce, or if the dog becomes ill? Are you willing to take back dogs you have bred? Also, what will happen to their puppies unless you have sold them on spay and neuter contracts?

We all know how many unfortunate dogs wind up put to death at the pound. Most Shih Tzu found in the animal shelters are the result of "commercial" breeding for wholesaling to pet shops and irresponsible "backyard" breeding by uneducated pet owners. Do you want to be responsible for adding to the statistics?

The best thing pet Shih Tzu owners can do for the breed is to have their pets spayed or neutered. Unaltered pets are more prone to develop mammary, prostatic and other forms of cancer. An altered pet is much easier to live with, and no dog needs to produce puppies to improve her temperament! One litter of puppies will cost you far more than a spay or neuter surgery, so do the right thing—for yourself, your dog and the breed.

If you *must* breed, *sell all your puppies on spay and neuter contracts.* Instead of breeding a litter, however, why not consider adopting a rescue dog or serving as a volunteer at your local animal shelter? The American Shih Tzu Club and many of the local breed clubs mentioned in Chapter 13 are active in Shih Tzu rescue and would welcome your help.

# Emergency First Aid

Certain emergencies, including shock, poisoning, prolonged seizure, coma, head injury, electric shock, choking, drowning, suffocation and sudden death may require that you administer **artificial respiration** and **cardiopulmonary resuscitation** (CPR). Administer artificial respiration to aid breathing in an unconscious dog. Use CPR when you cannot hear or feel a heartbeat.

**To administer artificial respiration**, put the dog on his side with his neck extended. After checking his mouth and clearing it of food or other obstructions, hold the muzzle closed and put your mouth over his nose. Slowly blow air into his nose for three seconds so that his chest expands, then release to allow the air to come out. Continue until the dog is breathing on his own or as long as his heart beats. If drowning has caused the problem, first suspend the dog upside down by his hind legs to allow the water to run out, and give artificial respiration with his head lower than his chest.

**To give CPR**, again place the dog on her side. Put your thumb on one side of her chest and your fingers on the other and compress her chest rapidly (about one hundred times per minute). Continue for five minutes, halting every thirty seconds to check whether her

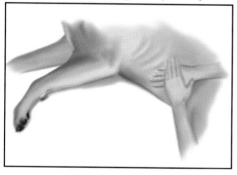

heartbeat has returned. For best results on a dog with no heartbeat, use two people and perform artificial respiration and CPR at the same time.

If the dog is **choking**, place a hard object between her molar teeth on one side of her mouth. With the

*Applying abdominal thrusts can save a choking dog.*

mouth thus held open, check for a foreign object at the back of the throat or tongue, roof of the mouth or between the teeth. Use long-nosed pliers to pull the body out. If you cannot remove it, hold your dog upside down by her hind legs and shake her to dislodge the object. If this does not work, use your fist to exert forceful, sudden pressure on the abdomen at the edge of the breastbone. If the dog is not breathing, administer artificial respiration.

When your dog has had prolonged exposure to cold, particularly if wet, she may suffer from **hypothermia**. Symptoms of hypothermia include violent shivering followed by listlessness and a rectal temperature below 97°F. Apply warm water packs to the armpit, chest and stomach or use a warm hair dryer until his temperature reaches 100°F, then give him honey to increase his blood sugar level.

**Heat stroke**, characterized by rapid, noisy breathing, a bright red tongue, thick saliva and sometimes vomiting, plus a high rectal temperature, requires immediate attention. Move the dog immediately to a cooler area. If her temperature is above 104°F, put her in a tub of cold water, hose her down with a garden hose or give her a cold water enema to bring her temperature down rapidly.

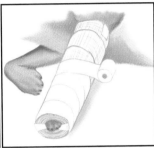

*Make a temporary splint by wrapping the leg in firm casing, then bandaging it.*

If the dog's vital organs are not receiving sufficient blood flow, she can go into **shock.** Her body temperature will drop, she will become listless and weak, her feet and legs will be cold, her skin will be pale and her pulse will be faint and weak. If the dog is not breathing, administer artificial respiration. If she has no heartbeat, administer CPR. Be sure the dog's airway is open, and control bleeding if necessary. Speak calmly to the dog, cover her with a coat or blanket and carry her to the veterinarian while protecting any injured parts.

In the case of **wounds**, the first thing to do is to stop the bleeding. Press sterile gauze pads firmly over the wound or, in the case of blood spurting from an artery, wrap a piece of cloth around the limb and tighten it until the bleeding is controlled. Loosen the tourniquet for a couple of minutes every fifteen minutes to let blood flow into the limb. In the case of broken bones, transport your dog to the veterinarian as quickly as possible, avoiding movement of the affected bones. If a wound is not severe enough to require veterinary attention, it must be cleaned once the bleeding has been stopped. Clip the hair around the wound, wash it with clean tap water, apply antibiotic ointment and bandage it to prevent further contamination.

In the case of **burns**, apply cold water soaks. Flush chemical burns with water. Then see your veterinarian. Also see your veterinarian if your dog becomes severely dehydrated. Signs of **dehydration** include dryness of the mouth, a lack of skin elasticity and sunken eyeballs.

*Give your Shih Tzu safe toys to play with and be careful she can't get into cabinets that contain toxic substances.*

If your dog has a sudden episode of **severe abdominal pain** coupled with vomiting and retching, it is an acute emergency requiring immediate veterinary attention. If your dog receives an **insect sting**, remove any stinger that remains with tweezers, apply a baking soda paste to the sting and use ice packs to relieve pain and swelling. Take her to your veterinarian if she has a severe allergic reaction to an insect sting.

## Poisoning

Among the most common household products causing poisoning in dogs are antifreeze (ethylene glycol), rat poison (anticoagulants such as wafarin and brodifacoum), matches and human drugs (including acetaminophen, aspirin, boric acid, phenol, sleeping pills and laxatives). Other ingredients in your medicine chest that could poison your dog include deodorants, hair colorings, nail polish and nail polish remover, permanent wave lotion, rubbing alcohol, soaps and suntan lotion.

Do not let your dog explore the cabinet under your kitchen sink—she could poison herself with bleach, cleaning fluid, deodorizers, detergent, disinfectant, drain cleaner, dye, furniture or metal polish, lye, moth-balls or shoe polish. In your garage, she might find brake fluid, carburetor cleaner, fungicides, herbicides, insecticides, gasoline, kerosene, lead, mineral spirits, paint, photographic developer, tar, turpentine, win-shield washer fluid or wood preservative.

A number of houseplants, including avocado, dieffen-bachia, English ivy, jasmine, philodendron and the bulbs of the amaryllis, daffodil, hyacinth, narcissus, iris and tulip are poisonous. So are apple seeds, cherry pits, chocolate, mushrooms, peaches, rhubarb, tobac-co and walnuts. At Christmas, be sure your dog does not ingest holly or mistletoe berries. Whatever mari-juana and jimson weed may do to your own health, they are definitely toxic to your dog!

When your dog is outside in your yard, do not let her eat andromeda, arrowgrass, azalea, bittersweet, box-wood, buttercups, caladium, castor beans, choke-cher-ry, climbing lily, crown of thorns, daphne, delphinium, dieffenbachia, dumb cane, elephant ear, elderberry, foxglove, hemlock, hydrangea, laburnum, larkspur, laurel, locoweed, marigold, monkshood, nightshade, oleander, poison ivy, privet, rhododendron, snow on the mountain, sting-ing nettle, toadstools, wisteria or yew.

*Some of the many house-hold substances harmful to your dog.*

The above listings are incomplete, but they include the most com-mon causes of poison-ing in dogs. To treat poisoning, it is impor-tant to know what your dog has ingested. If you have any questions, call the poison control hotline listed in Chapter 13.

In general, you should try to **induce vomiting** unless your dog has swallowed an acid, alkali, solvent, heavy duty cleanser, rodent poison or a petroleum product, any of which would severely damage the esophagus if vomited. Also induce vomiting if your dog has swallowed sharp objects or tranquilizers; if she is very depressed or comatose; or if the poison has been in the dog's system for more than two hours.

Induce vomiting by giving one teaspoon of three percent hydrogen peroxide every ten minutes three times or by placing one-half teaspoon of salt at the back of the tongue. Then give the dog one teaspoon per two pounds of body weight of one gram activated charcoal mixed with four cc's of water if it is available to delay or prevent the poison from being absorbed.

To speed elimination, give her one teaspoon of Milk of Magnesia per five pounds of body weight thirty minutes later. If your dog shows signs of nervous system involvement, get her to the veterinarian immediately.

# Caring for Your Older Shih Tzu

As your dog ages, she will spend more time sleeping. Because she is less active, she should consume fewer calories and still be given moderate exercise so that she does not become obese. Her hearing and eyesight may be less keen, her joints may become stiff and she may need to eliminate more frequently. The maintenance of her regular routine will provide her with needed security. If you notice any unusual behavior or symptoms, consult your veterinarian.

Shih Tzu are a long-lived breed. Most remain hale and hearty well into their teens. Sometimes, if introduced carefully, a young puppy can give an older dog a new lease on life. Just be sure that you do not neglect your old friend if you acquire a new puppy. Remember, the puppy has always been used to being one of a crowd, while your older dog needs to know that she still comes first in your life.

# Your Happy, Healthy Pet

Your Dog's Name _____

Name on Your Dog's Pedigree (if your dog has one) _____

_____

Where Your Dog Came From _____

_____

Your Dog's Birthday _____

Your Dog's Veterinarian

    Name    _____

    Address   _____

    Phone Number_____

    Emergency Number_____

Your Dog's Health

    Vaccines

    type _____ date given _____

    type _____ date given _____

    type _____ date given _____

    type _____ date given _____

    Heartworm

    date tested _____ type used_____ start date _____

Your Dog's License Number_____

Groomer's Name and Number _____

Dogsitter/Walker's Name and Number_____

Awards Your Dog Has Won

    Award _____ date earned _____

    Award _____ date earned _____

# Enjoying
## your
# Dog

# chapter 8

# Basic
# Training

*by Ian Dunbar, Ph.D., MRCVS*

Training is the jewel in the crown—the most important aspect of doggy husbandry. There is no more important variable influencing dog behavior and temperament than the dog's education: A well-trained, well-behaved and good-natured puppydog is always a joy to live with, but an untrained and uncivilized dog can be a perpetual nightmare. Moreover, deny the dog an education and she will not have the opportunity to fulfill her own canine potential; neither will she have the ability to communicate effectively with her human companions.

Luckily, modern psychological training methods are easy, efficient, effective and, above all, considerably dog-friendly and user-friendly.

Doggy education is as simple as it is enjoyable. But before you can have a good time play-training with your new dog, you have to learn what to do and how to do it. There is no bigger variable influencing the success of dog training than the *owner's* experience and expertise. *Before you embark on the dog's education, you must first educate yourself.*

# Basic Training for Owners

Ideally, basic owner training should begin well *before* you select your dog. Find out all you can about your chosen breed first, then master rudimentary training and handling skills. If you already have your puppy-dog, owner training is a dire emergency—the clock is ticking! Especially for puppies, the first few weeks at home are the most important and influential days in the dog's life. Indeed, the cause of most adolescent and adult problems may be traced back to the initial days the pup explores her new home. This is the time to establish the *status quo*—to teach the puppydog how you would like her to behave and so prevent otherwise quite predictable problems.

In addition to consulting breeders and breed books such as this one (which understandably have a positive breed bias), seek out as many pet owners with your breed as you can find. Good points are obvious. What you want to find out are the breed-specific *problems*, so you can nip them in the bud. In particular, you should talk to owners with *adolescent* dogs and make a list of all anticipated problems. Most important, *test drive* at least half a dozen adolescent and adult dogs of your breed yourself. An 8-week-old puppy is deceptively easy to handle, but she will acquire adult size, speed and strength in just four months, so you should learn now what to prepare for.

Puppy and pet dog training classes offer a convenient venue to locate pet owners and observe dogs in action. For a list of suitable trainers in your area, contact the Association of Pet Dog Trainers (see chapter 13). You may also begin your basic owner training by observing other owners in class. Watch as many classes and test drive as many dogs as possible. Select an upbeat, dog-friendly, people-friendly, fun-and-games, puppydog pet training class to learn the ropes. Also, watch training videos and read training books. You must find out what to do and how to do it *before* you have to do it.

# Principles of Training

Most people think training comprises teaching the dog to do things such as sit, speak and roll over, but even a 4-week-old pup knows how to do these things already. Instead, the first step in training involves teaching the dog human words for each dog behavior and activity and for each aspect of the dog's environment. That way you, the owner, can more easily participate in the dog's domestic education by directing her to perform specific actions appropriately, that is, at the right time, in the right place and so on. Training opens communication channels, enabling an educated dog to at least understand her owner's requests.

In addition to teaching a dog *what* we want her to do, it is also necessary to teach her *why* she should do what we ask. Indeed, 95 percent of training revolves around motivating the dog *to want to do* what we want. Dogs often understand what their owners want; they just don't see the point of doing it—especially when the owner's repetitively boring and seemingly senseless instructions are totally at odds with much more pressing and exciting doggy distractions. It is not so much the dog that is being stubborn or dominant; rather, it is the owner who has failed to acknowledge the dog's needs and feelings and to approach training from the dog's point of view.

## THE MEANING OF INSTRUCTIONS

The secret to successful training is learning how to use training lures to predict or prompt specific behaviors—to coax the dog to do what you want *when* you want. Any highly valued object (such as a treat or toy) may be used as a lure, which the dog will follow with her eyes and nose. Moving the lure in specific ways entices the dog to move her nose, head and entire body in specific ways. In fact, by learning the art of manipulating various lures, it is possible to teach the dog to assume virtually any body position and perform any action. Once you have control over the expression of the dog's behaviors and can elicit any body position or behavior at will, you can easily teach the dog to perform on request.

*Teach your dog words for each activity she needs to know, like down.*

Tell your dog what you want her to do, use a lure to entice her to respond correctly, then profusely praise and maybe reward her once she performs the desired action. For example, verbally request "Tina, sit!" while you move a squeaky toy upwards and backwards over the dog's muzzle (lure-movement and hand signal), smile knowingly as she looks up (to follow the lure) and sits down (as a result of canine anatomical engineering), then praise her to distraction ("Gooood Tina!"). Squeak the toy, offer a training treat and give your dog and yourself a pat on the back.

Being able to elicit desired responses over and over enables the owner to reward the dog over and over. Consequently, the dog begins to think training is fun. For example, the more the dog is rewarded for sitting, the more she enjoys sitting. Eventually the dog comes to realize that, whereas most sitting is appreciated, sitting immediately upon request usually prompts especially enthusiastic praise and a slew of high-level rewards. The dog begins to sit on cue much of the time, showing that she is starting to grasp the meaning of the owner's verbal request and hand signal.

## WHY COMPLY?

Most dogs enjoy initial lure-reward training and are only too happy to comply with their owners' wishes. Unfortunately, repetitive drilling without appreciative feedback tends to diminish the dog's enthusiasm until she eventually fails to see the point of complying anymore. Moreover, as the dog approaches adolescence she becomes more easily distracted as she develops other interests. Lengthy sessions with repetitive exercises tend to bore and demotivate both parties. If it's not fun, the owner doesn't do it and neither does the dog.

Integrate training into your dog's life: The greater number of training sessions each day and the *shorter* they are, the more willingly compliant your dog will

*To train your dog, you need gentle hands, a loving heart and a good attitude.*

become. Make sure to have a short (just a few seconds) training interlude before every enjoyable canine activity. For example, ask your dog to sit to greet people, to sit before you throw her Frisbee and to sit for her supper. Really, sitting is no different from a canine "Please."

Also, include numerous short training interludes during every enjoyable canine pastime, for example, when playing with the dog or when she is running in the park. In this fashion, doggy distractions may be effectively converted into rewards for training. Just as all games have rules, fun becomes training . . . and training becomes fun.

Eventually, rewards actually become unnecessary to continue motivating your dog. If trained with consideration and kindness, performing the desired behaviors will become self-rewarding and, in a sense, your dog will motivate herself. Just as it is not necessary to reward a human companion during an enjoyable walk in the park, or following a game of tennis, it is hardly necessary to reward our best friend—the dog— for walking by our side or while playing fetch. Human company during enjoyable activities is reward enough for most dogs.

Even though your dog has become self-motivating, it's still good to praise and pet her a lot and offer rewards once in a while, especially for a good job well done. And if for no other reason, praising and rewarding others is good for the human heart.

## PUNISHMENT

Without a doubt, lure-reward training is by far the best way to teach: Entice your dog to do what you want and then reward her for doing so. Unfortunately, a human shortcoming is to take the good for granted and to moan and groan at the bad. Specifically, the dog's many good behaviors are ignored while the owner focuses on punishing the dog for making mistakes. In extreme cases, instruction is *limited* to punishing mistakes made by a trainee dog, child, employee or husband, even though it has been proven punishment training is notoriously inefficient and ineffective and is decidedly unfriendly and combative. It teaches the dog that training is a drag, almost as quickly as it teaches the dog to dislike her trainer. Why treat our best friends like our worst enemies?

Punishment training is also much more laborious and time consuming. Whereas it takes only a finite amount of time to teach a dog what to chew, for example, it takes much, much longer to punish the dog for each and every mistake. Remember, *there is only one right way!* So why not teach that right way from the outset?!

103

To make matters worse, punishment training causes severe lapses in the dog's reliability. Since it is obviously impossible to punish the dog each and every time she misbehaves, the dog quickly learns to distinguish between those times when she must comply (so as to avoid impending punishment) and those times when she need not comply, because punishment is impossible. Such times include when the dog is off leash and 6 feet away, when the owner is otherwise engaged (talking to a friend, watching television, taking a shower, tending to the baby or chatting on the telephone) or when the dog is left at home alone.

Instances of misbehavior will be numerous when the owner is away, because even when the dog complied in the owner's looming presence, she did so unwillingly. The dog was forced to act against her will, rather than molding her will to want to please. Hence, when the owner is absent, not only does the dog know she need not comply, she simply does not want to. Again, the trainee is not a stubborn vindictive beast, but rather the trainer has failed to teach. Punishment training invariably creates unpredictable Jekyll and Hyde behavior.

## Trainer's Tools

Many training books extol the virtues of a vast array of training paraphernalia and electronic and metallic gizmos, most of which are designed for canine restraint, correction and punishment, rather than for actual facilitation of doggy education. In reality, most effective training tools are not found in stores; they come from within ourselves. In addition to a willing dog, all you really need is a functional human brain, gentle hands, a loving heart and a good attitude.

In terms of equipment, all dogs do require a quality buckle collar to sport dog tags and to attach the leash (for safety and to comply with local leash laws). Hollow chew toys (like Kongs or sterilized longbones) and a dog bed or collapsible crate are musts for housetraining. Three additional tools are required:

If your dog does not eliminate within the allotted time outside—no biggie! Back to her doggy den, and then try again after another hour.

As I own large dogs, I always feel more relaxed walking an empty dog, knowing that I will not need to finish our stroll weighted down with bags of feces!

Beware of falling into the trap of walking the dog to get her to eliminate. The good ol' dog walk is such an enormous highlight in the dog's life that it represents the single biggest potential reward in domestic dogdom. However, when in a hurry, or during inclement weather, many owners abruptly terminate the walk the moment the dog has done her business. This, in effect, severely punishes the dog for doing the right thing, in the right place at the right time. Consequently, many dogs become strongly inhibited from eliminating outdoors because they know it will signal an abrupt end to an otherwise thoroughly enjoyable walk.

Instead, instruct the dog to relieve herself in the yard prior to going for a walk. If you follow the above instructions, most dogs soon learn to eliminate on cue. As soon as the dog eliminates, praise (and offer a treat or two)—"Good dog! Let's go walkies!" Use the walk as a reward for eliminating in the yard. If the dog does not go, put her back in her doggy den and think about a walk later on. You will find with a "No feces—no walk" policy, your dog will become one of the fastest defecators in the business.

If you do not have a backyard, instruct the dog to eliminate right outside your front door prior to the walk. Not only will this facilitate clean up and disposal of the feces in your own trash can but, also, the walk may again be used as a colossal reward.

## Chewing and Barking

Short-term close confinement also teaches the dog that occasional quiet moments are a reality of domestic living. Your puppydog is extremely impressionable during her first few weeks at home. Regular confinement at this time soon exerts a calming influence over the dog's personality. Remember, once the dog is housetrained and calmer, there will be a whole lifetime ahead for the dog to enjoy full run of the house and garden. On the other hand, by letting the newcomer have unrestricted access to the entire household and allowing her to run willy-nilly, she will most certainly develop a bunch of behavior problems in short order, no doubt necessitating confinement later in life. It would not be fair to remedially restrain and confine a dog you have trained, through neglect, to run free.

When confining the dog, make sure she always has an impressive array of suitable chew toys. Kongs and sterilized longbones (both readily available from pet stores) make the best chew toys, since they are hollow and may be stuffed with treats to heighten the dog's interest. For example, by stuffing the little hole at the top of a Kong with a small piece of freeze-dried liver, the dog will not want to leave it alone.

Remember, treats do not have to be junk food and they certainly should not represent extra calories. Rather, treats should be part of each dog's regular daily diet: Some food may be served in the dog's bowl for breakfast and dinner, some food may be used as training treats, and some food may be used for stuffing chew toys. I regularly stuff my dogs' many Kongs with different shaped biscuits and kibble.

*Make sure your puppy has suitable chew toys.*

The kibble seems to fall out fairly easily, as do the oval-shaped biscuits, thus rewarding the dog instantaneously for checking out the chew toys. The bone-shaped biscuits fall out after a while, rewarding the dog for worrying at the chew toy. But the triangular biscuits never come out. They remain inside the Kong as lures, maintaining the dog's fascination with her chew toy. To further focus the dog's interest, I always make sure to flavor the triangular biscuits by rubbing them with a little cheese or freeze-dried liver.

*To teach come, call your dog, open your arms as a welcoming signal, wave a toy or a treat and praise for every step in your direction.*

If stuffed chew toys are reserved especially for times the dog is confined, the puppydog will soon learn to enjoy quiet moments in her doggy den and she will quickly develop a chew-toy habit—a good habit! This is a simple *autoshaping* process; all the owner has to do is set up the situation and the dog all but trains herself—easy and effective. Even when the dog is given run of the house, her first inclination will be to indulge her rewarding chew-toy habit rather than destroy less-attractive household articles, such as curtains, carpets, chairs and compact disks. Similarly, a chew-toy chewer will be less inclined to scratch and chew herself excessively. Also, if the dog busies herself as a recreational chewer, she will be less inclined to develop into a recreational barker or digger when left at home alone.

Stuff a number of chew toys whenever the dog is left confined and remove the extra-special-tasting treats when you return. Your dog will now amuse herself with her chew toys before falling asleep and then resume playing with her chew toys when she expects you to return. Since most owner-absent misbehavior happens right after you leave and right before your expected return, your puppydog will now be conveniently preoccupied with her chew toys at these times.

## Come and Sit

Most puppies will happily approach virtually anyone, whether called or not; that is, until they collide with adolescence and

develop other more important doggy interests, such as sniffing a multiplicity of exquisite odors on the grass. Your mission, Mr./Ms. Owner, is to teach and reward the pup for coming reliably, willingly and happily when called—and you have just three months to get it done. Unless adequately reinforced, your puppy's tendency to approach people will self-destruct by adolescence.

Call your dog ("Tina, come!"), open your arms (and maybe squat down) as a welcoming signal, waggle a treat or toy as a lure and reward the puppydog when she comes running. Do not wait to praise the dog until she reaches you—she may come 95 percent of the way and then run off after some distraction. Instead, praise the dog's *first* step towards you and continue praising enthusiastically for *every* step she takes in your direction.

When the rapidly approaching puppy dog is three lengths away from impact, instruct her to sit ("Tina, sit!") and hold the lure in front of you in an outstretched hand to prevent her from hitting you mid-chest and knocking you flat on your back! As Tina decelerates to nose the lure, move the treat upwards and backwards just over her muzzle with an upwards motion of your extended arm (palm-upwards). As the dog looks up to follow the lure, she will sit down (if she jumps up, you are holding the lure too high). Praise the dog for sitting. Move backwards and call her again. Repeat this many times over, always praising when Tina comes and sits; on occasion, reward her.

For the first couple of trials, use a training treat both as a lure to entice the dog to come and sit and as a reward for doing so. Thereafter, try to use different items as lures and rewards. For example, lure the dog with a Kong or Frisbee but reward her with a food treat. Or lure the dog with a food treat but pat her and throw a tennis ball as a reward. After just a few repetitions, dispense with the lures and rewards; the dog will begin to respond willingly to your verbal requests and hand signals just for the prospect of praise from your heart and affection from your hands.

Instruct every family member, friend and visitor how to get the dog to come and sit. Invite people over for a series of pooch parties; do not keep the pup a secret—let other people enjoy this puppy, and let the pup enjoy other people. Puppydog parties are not only fun, they easily attract a lot of people to help *you* train *your* dog. Unless you teach your dog how to meet people, that is, to sit for greetings, no doubt the dog will resort to jumping up. Then you and the visitors will get annoyed, and the dog will be punished. This is not fair. *Send out those invitations for puppy parties and teach your dog to be mannerly and socially acceptable.*

Even though your dog quickly masters obedient recalls in the house, her reliability may falter when playing in the backyard or local park. Ironically, it is *the owner* who has unintentionally trained the dog *not* to respond in these instances. By allowing the dog to play and run around and otherwise have a good time, but then to call the dog to put her on leash to take her home, the dog quickly learns playing is fun but training is a drag. Thus, playing in the park becomes a severe distraction, which works against training. Bad news!

Instead, whether playing with the dog off leash or on leash, request her to come at frequent intervals—say, every minute or so. On most occasions, praise and pet the dog for a few seconds while she is sitting, then tell her to go play again. For especially fast recalls, offer a couple of training treats and take the time to praise and pet the dog enthusiastically before releasing her. The dog will learn that coming when called is not necessarily the end of the play session, and neither is it the end of the world; rather, it signals an enjoyable, quality time-out with the owner before resuming play once more. In fact, playing in the park now becomes a very effective life-reward, which works to facilitate training by reinforcing each obedient and timely recall. Good news!

# Sit, Down, Stand and Rollover

Teaching the dog a variety of body positions is easy for owner and dog, impressive for spectators and extremely useful for all. Using lure-reward techniques, it is possible to train several positions at once to verbal commands or hand signals (which impress the socks off onlookers).

*Sit* and ***down***—the two control commands—prevent or resolve nearly a hundred behavior problems. For example, if the dog happily and obediently sits or lies down when requested, she cannot jump on visitors, dash out the front door, run around and chase her tail, pester other dogs, harass cats or annoy family, friends or strangers. Additionally, "Sit" or "Down" are the best emergency commands for off-leash control.

It is easier to teach and maintain a reliable sit than maintain a reliable recall. *Sit* is the purest and simplest of commands—either the dog is sitting or she is not. If there is any change of circumstances or potential danger in the park, for example, simply instruct the dog to sit. If she sits, you have a number of options: Allow the dog to resume playing when she is safe, walk up and put the dog on leash or call the dog. The dog will be much more likely to come when called if she has already acknowledged her compliance by sitting. If the dog does not sit in the park—train her to!

*Stand* and *rollover-stay* are the two positions for examining the dog. Your veterinarian will love you to distraction if you take a little time to teach the dog to stand still and roll over and play possum. Also, your vet bills will be smaller because it will take the veterinarian less time to examine your dog. The rollover-stay is an especially useful command and is really just a variation of the down-stay: Whereas the dog lies prone in the traditional down, she lies supine in the rollover-stay.

As with teaching come and sit, the training techniques to teach the dog to assume all other body positions on cue are user-friendly and dog-friendly. Simply give the appropriate request, lure the dog into the desired body position using a training treat or toy and then *praise* (and maybe reward) the dog as soon as she complies. Try not to touch the dog to get her to respond. If you teach the dog by guiding her into position, the dog will quickly learn that rump-pressure means sit, for example, but as yet you still have no control over your dog if she is just 6 feet away. It will still be necessary to teach the dog to sit on request. So do not make training a time-consuming two-step process; instead, teach the dog to sit to a verbal request or hand signal from the outset. Once the dog sits willingly when requested, by all means use your hands to pet the dog when she does so.

To teach **down** when the dog is already sitting, say "Tina, down!," hold the lure in one hand (palm down) and lower that hand to the floor between the dog's forepaws. As the dog lowers her head to follow the lure, slowly move the lure away from the dog just a fraction (in front of her paws). The dog will lie down as she stretches her nose forward to follow the lure. Praise the dog when she does so. If the dog stands up, you pulled the lure away too far and too quickly.

When teaching the dog to lie down from the standing position, say "Down" and lower the lure to the floor as before. Once the dog has lowered her forequarters and assumed a play bow, gently and slowly move the lure *towards* the dog between her forelegs. Praise the dog as soon as her rear end plops down.

After just a couple of trials it will be possible to alternate sits and downs and have the dog energetically perform doggy push-ups. Praise the dog a lot, and after half a dozen or so push-ups reward the dog with a training treat or toy. You will notice the more energetically you move your arm—upwards (palm up) to get the dog to sit, and downwards (palm down) to get the dog to lie down—the more energetically the dog responds to your requests. Now try training the dog in silence and you will notice she has also learned to respond to hand signals. Yeah! Not too shabby for the first session.

To teach **stand** from the sitting position, say "Tina, stand," slowly move the lure half a dog-length away from the dog's nose, keeping it at nose level, and praise the dog as she stands to follow the lure. As soon

*Using a food lure to teach sit, down and stand. 1) "Phoenix, sit." 2) Hand palm upwards, move lure up and back over dog's muzzle. 3) "Good sit, Phoenix!" 4) "Phoenix, down." 5) Hand palm downwards, move lure down to lie between dog's forepaws. 6) "Phoenix, off. Good down, Phoenix!" 7) "Phoenix, sit!" 8) Palm upwards, move lure up and back, keeping it close to dog's muzzle. 9) "Good sit, Phoenix!"*

*10) "Phoenix, stand!" 11) Move lure away from dog at nose height, then lower it a tad. 12) "Phoenix, off! Good stand, Phoenix!" 13) "Phoenix, down!" 14) Hand palm downwards, move lure down to lie between dog's forepaws. 15) "Phoenix, off! Good down-stay, Phoenix!" 16) "Phoenix, stand!" 17) Move lure away from dog's muzzle up to nose height. 18) "Phoenix, off! Good stand-stay, Phoenix. Now we'll make the vet and groomer happy!"*

as the dog stands, lower the lure to just beneath the dog's chin to entice her to look down; otherwise she will stand and then sit immediately. To prompt the dog to stand from the down position, move the lure half a dog-length upwards and away from the dog, holding the lure at standing nose height from the floor.

Teaching **rollover** is best started from the down position, with the dog lying on one side, or at least with both hind legs stretched out on the same side. Say "Tina, bang!" and move the lure backwards and alongside the dog's muzzle to her elbow (on the side of her outstretched hind legs). Once the dog looks to the side and backwards, very slowly move the lure upwards to the dog's shoulder and backbone. Tickling the dog in the goolies (groin area) often invokes a reflex-raising of the hind leg as an appeasement gesture, which facilitates the tendency to roll over. If you move the lure too quickly and the dog jumps into the standing position, have patience and start again. As soon as the dog rolls onto her back, keep the lure stationary and mesmerize the dog with a relaxing tummy rub.

To teach **rollover-stay** when the dog is standing or moving, say "Tina, bang!" and give the appropriate hand signal (with index finger pointed and thumb cocked in true Sam Spade fashion), then in one fluid movement lure her to first lie down and then rollover-stay as above.

Teaching the dog to **stay** in each of the above four positions becomes a piece of cake after first teaching the dog not to worry at the toy or treat training lure. This is best accomplished by hand feeding dinner kibble. Hold a piece of kibble firmly in your hand and softly instruct "Off!" Ignore any licking and slobbering *for however long the dog worries at the treat*, but say "Take it!" and offer the kibble *the instant* the dog breaks contact with her muzzle. Repeat this a few times, and then up the ante and insist the dog remove her muzzle for one whole second before offering the kibble. Then progressively refine your criteria and have the dog not touch your hand (or treat) for longer and longer periods on each trial, such as for two seconds, four seconds, then six, ten, fifteen, twenty, thirty seconds and so on.

The dog soon learns: (1) worrying at the treat never gets results, whereas (2) noncontact is often rewarded after a variable time lapse.

Teaching *"Off!"* has many useful applications in its own right. Additionally, instructing the dog not to touch a training lure often produces spontaneous and magical stays. Request the dog to stand-stay, for example, and not to touch the lure. At first set your sights on a short two-second stay before rewarding the dog. (Remember, every long journey begins with a single step.) However, on subsequent trials, gradually and progressively increase the length of stay required to receive a reward. In no time at all your dog will stand calmly for a minute or so.

# Relevancy Training

Once you have taught the dog what you expect her to do when requested to come, sit, lie down, stand, rollover and stay, the time is right to teach the dog *why* she should comply with your wishes. The secret is to have many (*many*) extremely short training interludes (two to five seconds each) at numerous (*numerous*) times during the course of the dog's day. Especially work with the dog immediately *before* the dog's good times and *during* the dog's good times. For example, ask your dog to sit and/or lie down each time before opening doors, serving meals, offering treats and tummy rubs; ask the dog to perform a few controlled doggy push-ups before letting her off leash or throwing a tennis ball; and perhaps request the dog to sit-down-sit-stand-down-stand-rollover before inviting her to cuddle on the couch.

Similarly, request the dog to sit many times during play or on walks, and in no time at all the dog will be only too pleased to follow your instructions because she has learned that a compliant response heralds all sorts of goodies. Basically all you are trying to teach the dog is how to say please: "Please throw the tennis ball. Please may I snuggle on the couch."

Remember, it is important to keep training interludes short and to have many short sessions each and every day. The shortest (and most useful) session comprises asking the dog to sit and then go play during a play session. When trained this way, your dog will soon associate training with good times. In fact, the dog may be unable to distinguish between training and good times and, indeed, there should be no distinction. The warped concept that training involves forcing the dog to comply and/or dominating her will is totally at odds with the picture of a truly well-trained dog. In reality, enjoying a game of training with a dog is no different from enjoying a game of backgammon or tennis with a friend; and walking with a dog should be no different from strolling with a spouse, or with buddies on the golf course.

# Walk by Your Side

Many people attempt to teach a dog to heel by putting her on a leash and physically correcting the dog when she makes mistakes. There are a number of things seriously wrong with this approach, the first being that most people do not want precision heeling; rather, they simply want the dog to follow or walk by their side. Second, when physically restrained during "training," even though the dog may grudgingly mope by your side when "handcuffed" on leash, let's see what happens when she is off leash. History! The dog is in the next county because she never enjoyed walking with you on leash and you have no control over her off leash. So let's just teach the dog off leash from the outset to *want* to walk with us. Third, if the dog has not been trained to heel, it is a trifle hasty to think about punishing the poor dog for making mistakes and breaking heeling rules she didn't even know existed. This is simply not fair! Surely, if the dog had been adequately taught how to heel, she would seldom make mistakes and hence there would be no need to correct the dog. Remember, each mistake and each correction (punishment) advertise the trainer's inadequacy, not the dog's. The dog is not stubborn, she is not stupid and she is not bad. Even if she were, she would still require training, so let's train her properly.

Let's teach the dog to *enjoy* following us and to *want* to walk by our side off leash. Then it will be easier to teach high-precision off-leash heeling patterns if desired. Before going on outdoor walks, it is necessary to teach the dog not to pull. Then it becomes easy to teach on-leash walking and heeling because the dog already wants to walk with you, she is familiar with the desired walking and heeling positions and she knows not to pull.

## FOLLOWING

Start by training your dog to follow you. Many puppies will follow if you simply walk away from them and maybe click your fingers or chuckle. Adult dogs may require additional enticement to stimulate them to follow, such as a training lure or, at the very least, a lively trainer. To teach the dog to follow: (1) keep walking and (2) walk away from the dog. If the dog attempts to lead or lag, change pace; slow down if the dog forges too far ahead, but speed up if she lags too far behind. Say "Steady!" or "Easy!" each time before you slow down and "Quickly!" or "Hustle!" each time before you speed up, and the dog will learn to change pace on cue. If the dog lags or leads too far, or if she wanders right or left, simply walk quickly in the opposite direction and maybe even run away from the dog and hide.

Practicing is a lot of fun; you can set up a course in your home, yard or park to do this. Indoors, entice the dog to follow upstairs, into a bedroom, into the bathroom, downstairs, around the living room couch, zigzagging between dining room chairs and into the kitchen for dinner. Outdoors, get the dog to follow around park benches, trees, shrubs and along walkways and lines in the grass. (For safety outdoors, it is advisable to attach a long line on the dog, but never exert corrective tension on the line.)

Remember, following has a lot to do with attitude—
*your* attitude! Most probably your dog will *not* want to
follow Mr. Grumpy Troll with the personality of wilted
lettuce. Lighten up—walk with a jaunty step, whistle a
happy tune, sing, skip and tell jokes to your dog and
she will be right there by your side.

## BY YOUR SIDE

It is smart to train the dog to walk close on one side or
the other—either side will do, your choice. When walking, jogging or cycling, it is generally bad news to have
the dog suddenly cut in front of you. In fact, I train my
dogs to walk "By my side" and "Other side"—both very
useful instructions. It is possible to position the dog
fairly accurately by looking to the appropriate side and
clicking your fingers or slapping your thigh on that
side. A precise positioning may be attained by holding
a training lure, such as a chew toy, tennis ball or food
treat. Stop and stand still several times throughout the
walk, just as you would when window shopping or
meeting a friend. Use the lure to make sure the dog
slows down and stays close whenever you stop.

When teaching the dog to heel, we generally want
her to sit in heel position when we stop. Teach heel

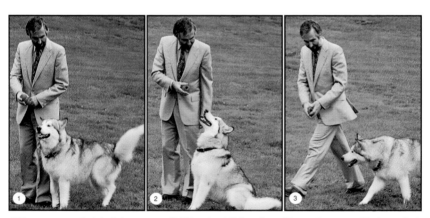

*Using a toy to teach sit-heel-sit sequences: 1) "Phoenix, sit!" Standing still, move lure up and back over dog's muzzle . . . 2) to position dog sitting in heel position on your left side. 3) Say "Phoenix, heel!" and walk ahead, wagging lure in left hand. Change lure to right hand in preparation for sit signal. Say "Sit" and then . . .*

position at the standstill and the dog will learn that the default heel position is sitting by your side (left or right—your choice, unless you wish to compete in obedience trials, in which case the dog must heel on the left).

Several times a day, stand up and call your dog to come and sit in heel position—"Tina, heel!" For example, instruct the dog to come to heel each time there are commercials on TV, or each time you turn a page of a novel, and the dog will get it in a single evening.

Practice straight-line heeling and turns separately. With the dog sitting at heel, teach her to turn in place. After each quarter-turn, half-turn or full turn in place, lure the dog to sit at heel. Now it's time for short straight-line heeling sequences, no more than a few steps at a time. Always think of heeling in terms of sit-heel-sit sequences—start and end with the dog in position and do your best to keep her there when moving. Progressively increase the number of steps in each sequence. When the dog remains close for 20 yards of straight-line heeling, it is time to add a few turns and then sign up for a happy-heeling obedience class to get some advice from the experts.

*4) use hand signal to lure dog to sit as you stop. Eventually, dog will sit automatically at heel whenever you stop. 5) "Good dog!"*

# No Pulling on Leash

You can start teaching your dog not to pull on leash anywhere—in front of the television or outdoors—but regardless of location, you must not take a single step with tension in the leash. For a reason known only to dogs, even just a couple of paces of pulling on leash is intrinsically motivating and diabolically rewarding. Instead, attach the leash to the dog's collar, grasp the other end firmly with both hands held close to your chest, and stand still—do not budge an inch. Have somebody watch you with a stopwatch to time your progress, or else you will never believe this will work and so you will not even try the exercise, and your shoulder and the dog's neck will be traumatized for years to come.

Stand still and wait for the dog to stop pulling, and to sit and/or lie down. All dogs stop pulling and sit eventually. Most take only a couple of minutes; the all-time record is 22½ minutes. Time how long it takes. Gently praise the dog when she stops pulling, and as soon as she sits, enthusiastically praise the dog and take just one step forward, then immediately stand still. This single step usually demonstrates the ballistic reinforcing nature of pulling on leash; most dogs explode to the end of the leash, so be prepared for the strain. Stand firm and wait for the dog to sit again. Repeat this half a dozen times and you will probably notice a progressive reduction in the force of the dog's one-step explosions and a radical reduction in the time it takes for the dog to sit each time.

As the dog learns "Sit we go" and "Pull we stop," she will begin to walk forward calmly with each single step and automatically sit when you stop. Now try two steps before you stop. Wooooooo! Scary! When the dog has mastered two steps at a time, try for three. After each success, progressively increase the number of steps in the sequence: try four steps and then six, eight, ten and twenty steps before stopping. Congratulations! You are now walking the dog on leash.

Whenever walking with the dog (off leash or on leash), make sure you stop periodically to practice a few position commands and stays before instructing the dog to "Walk on!" (Remember, you want the dog to be compliant everywhere, not just in the kitchen when her dinner is at hand.) For example, stopping every 25 yards to briefly train the dog amounts to over 200 training interludes within a single 3-mile stroll. And each training session is in a different location. You will not believe the improvement within just the first mile of the first walk.

To put it another way, integrating training into a walk offers 200 separate opportunities to use the continuance of the walk as a reward to reinforce the dog's education. Moreover, some training interludes may comprise continuing education for the dog's walking skills: Alternate short periods of the dog walking calmly by your side with periods when the dog is allowed to sniff and investigate the environment. Now sniffing odors on the grass and meeting other dogs become rewards which reinforce the dog's calm and mannerly demeanor. Good Lord! Whatever next? Many enjoyable walks together of course. Happy trails!

# THE IMPORTANCE OF TRICKS

Nothing will improve a dog's quality of life better than having a few tricks under her belt. Teaching any trick expands the dog's vocabulary, which facilitates communication and improves the owner's control. Also, specific tricks help prevent and resolve specific behavior problems. For example, by teaching the dog to fetch her toys, the dog learns carrying a toy makes the owner happy and, therefore, will be more likely to chew her toy than other inappropriate items.

More important, teaching tricks prompts owners to lighten up and train with a sunny disposition. Really, tricks should be no different from any other behaviors we put on cue. But they are. When teaching tricks, owners have a much sweeter attitude, which in turn motivates the dog and improves her willingness to comply. The dog feels tricks are a blast, but formal commands are a drag. In fact, tricks are so enjoyable, they may be used as rewards in training by asking the dog to come, sit and down-stay and then rollover for a tummy rub. Go on, try it: Crack a smile and even giggle when the dog promptly and willingly lies down and stays.

Most important, performing tricks prompts onlookers to smile and gig-gle. Many people are scared of dogs, especially large ones. And noth-ing can be more off-putting for a dog than to be constantly confronted by strangers who don't like her because of her size or the way she looks. Uneasy people put the dog on edge, causing her to back off and bark, only frightening people all the more. And so a vicious circle devel-ops, with the people's fear fueling the dog's fear *and vice versa*. Instead, tie a pink ribbon to your dog's collar and practice all sorts of tricks on walks and in the park, and you will be pleasantly amazed how it changes people's attitudes toward your friendly dog. The dog's reper-toire of tricks is limited only by the trainer's imagination. Below I have described three of my favorites:

### SPEAK AND SHUSH

The training sequence involved in teaching a dog to bark on request is no different from that used when training any behavior on cue: request—lure—response—reward. As always, the secret of success lies in finding an effective lure. If the dog always barks at the doorbell, for example, say "Rover, speak!", have an accomplice ring the doorbell, then reward the dog for barking. After a few woofs, ask Rover to "Shush!", waggle a food treat under her nose (to entice her to sniff and thus to shush), praise her when quiet and eventually offer the treat as a reward. Alternate "Speak" and "Shush," progressively increasing the length of shush-time between each barking bout.

### PLAY BOW

With the dog standing, say "Bow!" and lower the food lure (palm upwards) to rest between the dog's forepaws. Praise as the dog lowers her forequarters and sternum to the ground (as when teaching the down), but then lure the dog to stand and offer the treat. On successive trials, gradually increase the length of time the dog is required to remain in the play bow posture in order to gain a food reward. If the dog's rear end collapses into a down, say nothing and offer no reward; simply start over.

### BE A BEAR

With the dog sitting backed into a corner to prevent her from toppling over backwards, say "Be a bear!" With bent paw and palm down, raise a lure upwards and backwards along the top of the dog's muzzle. Praise the dog when she sits up on her haunches and offer the treat as a reward. To prevent the dog from standing on her hind legs, keep the lure closer to the dog's muzzle. On each trial, progressively increase the length of time the dog is required to sit up to receive a food reward. Since lure-reward training is so easy, teach the dog to stand and walk on her hind legs as well!

*Teaching "Be a Bear"*

127

# chapter 9

# Getting
# Active
## with your Dog

*by Bardi McLennan*

Once you and your dog have graduated from basic obedience training and are beginning to work together as a team, you can take part in the growing world of dog activities. There are so many fun things to do with your dog! Just remember, people and dogs don't always learn at the same pace, so don't be upset if you (or your dog) need more than two basic training courses before your team becomes operational. Even smart dogs don't go straight to college from kindergarten!

Just as there are events geared to certain types of dogs, so there are ones that are more appealing to certain types of people. In some activities, you give the commands and your dog does the work (upland game hunting is one example), while in others, such as agility, you'll both get a workout. You may want to aim for prestigious titles to add to your dog's name, or you may want nothing more than the sheer enjoyment of being around other people and their dogs. Passive or active, participation has its own rewards.

Consider your dog's physical capabilities when looking into any of the canine activities. It's easy to see that a Basset Hound is not built for the racetrack, nor would a Chihuahua be the breed of choice for pulling a sled. A loyal dog will attempt almost anything you ask him to do, so it is up to you to know your dog's limitations. A dog must be physically sound in order to compete at any level in athletic activities, and being mentally sound is a definite plus. Advanced age, however, may not be a deterrent. Many dogs still hunt and herd at ten or twelve years of age. It's entirely possible for dogs to be "fit at 50." Take your dog for a checkup, explain to your vet the type of activity you have in mind and be guided by his or her findings.

*All dogs seem to love playing flyball.*

You needn't be restricted to breed-specific sports if it's only fun you're after. Certain AKC activities are limited to designated breeds; however, as each new trial, test or sport has grown in popularity, so has the variety of breeds encouraged to participate at a fun level.

But don't shortchange your fun, or that of your dog, by thinking only of the basic function of her breed. Once a dog has learned how to learn, she can be taught to do just about anything as long as the size of the dog is right for the job and you both think it is fun and rewarding. In other words, you are a team.

To get involved in any of the activities detailed in this chapter, look for the names and addresses of the organizations that sponsor them in Chapter 13. You can also ask your breeder or a local dog trainer for contacts.

*You can compete in obedience trials with a well trained dog.*

# Official American Kennel Club Activities

The following tests and trials are some of the events sanctioned by the AKC and sponsored by various dog clubs. Your dog's expertise will be rewarded with impressive titles. You can participate just for fun, or be competitive and go for those awards.

## OBEDIENCE

Training classes begin with pups as young as three months of age in kindergarten puppy training, then advance to pre-novice (all exercises on lead) and go on to novice, which is where you'll start off-lead work. In obedience classes dogs learn to sit, stay, heel and come through a variety of exercises. Once you've got the basics down, you can enter obedience trials and work toward earning your dog's first degree, a C.D. (Companion Dog).

The next level is called "Open," in which jumps and retrieves perk up the dog's interest. Passing grades in competition at this level earn a C.D.X. (Companion Dog Excellent). Beyond that lies the goal of the most ambitious—Utility (U.D. and even U.D.X. or OTCh, an Obedience Champion).

## AGILITY

All dogs can participate in the latest canine sport to have gained worldwide popularity for its fun and excitement, agility. It began in England as a canine version of horse show-jumping, but because dogs are more agile and able to perform on verbal commands, extra feats were added such as climbing, balancing and racing through tunnels or in and out of weave poles. Many of the obstacles (regulation or homemade) can be set up in your own backyard. If the agility bug bites, you could end up in international competition!

For starters, your dog should be obedience trained, even though, in the beginning, the lessons may all be taught on lead. Once the dog understands the commands (and you do, too), it's as easy as guiding the dog over a prescribed course, one obstacle at a time. In competition, the race is against the clock, so wear your running shoes! The dog starts with 200 points and the judge deducts for infractions and misadventures along the way.

All dogs seem to love agility and respond to it as if they were being turned loose in a playground paradise. Your dog's enthusiasm will be contagious; agility turns into great fun for dog and owner.

## FIELD TRIALS AND HUNTING TESTS

There are field trials and hunting tests for the sporting breeds—retrievers, spaniels and pointing breeds, and for some hounds—Bassets, Beagles and Dachshunds. Field trials are competitive events that test a dog's ability to perform the functions for which she was bred. Hunting tests, which are open to retrievers,

---

### TITLES AWARDED BY THE AKC

*Conformation*: Ch. (Champion)

*Obedience*: CD (Companion Dog); CDX (Companion Dog Excellent); UD (Utility Dog); UDX (Utility Dog Excellent); OTCh. (Obedience Trial Champion)

*Field*: JH (Junior Hunter); SH (Senior Hunter); MH (Master Hunter); AFCh. (Amateur Field Champion); FCh. (Field Champion)

*Lure Coursing*: JC (Junior Courser); SC (Senior Courser)

*Herding*: HT (Herding Tested); PT (Pre-Trial Tested); HS (Herding Started); HI (Herding Intermediate); HX (Herding Excellent); HCh. (Herding Champion)

*Tracking*: TD (Tracking Dog); TDX (Tracking Dog Excellent)

*Agility*: NAD (Novice Agility); OAD (Open Agility); ADX (Agility Excellent); MAX (Master Agility)

*Earthdog Tests*: JE (Junior Earthdog); SE (Senior Earthdog); ME (Master Earthdog)

*Canine Good Citizen*: CGC

*Combination*: DC (Dual Champion—Ch. and Fch.); TC (Triple Champion—Ch., Fch., and OTCh.)

spaniels and pointing breeds only, are noncompetitive and are a means of judging the dog's ability as well as that of the handler.

Hunting is a very large and complex part of canine sports, and if you own one of the breeds that hunts, the events are a great treat for your dog and you. He gets to do what he was bred for, and you get to work with him and watch him do it. You'll be proud of and amazed at what your dog can do.

Fortunately, the AKC publishes a series of booklets on these events, which outline the rules and regulations and include a glossary of the sometimes complicated terms. The AKC also publishes newsletters for field trialers and hunting test enthusiasts. The United Kennel Club (UKC) also has informative materials for the hunter and his dog.

*Retrievers and other sporting breeds get to do what they're bred to in hunting tests.*

## HERDING TESTS AND TRIALS

Herding, like hunting, dates back to the first known uses man made of dogs. The interest in herding today is widespread, and if you own a herding breed, you can join in the activity. Herding dogs are tested for their natural skills to keep a flock of ducks, sheep or cattle together. If your dog shows potential, you can start at the testing level, where your dog can earn a title for showing an inherent herding ability. With training you can advance to the trial level, where your dog should be capable of controlling even difficult livestock in diverse situations.

## LURE COURSING

The AKC Tests and Trials for Lure Coursing are open to traditional sighthounds—Greyhounds, Whippets,

Borzoi, Salukis, Afghan Hounds, Ibizan Hounds and Scottish Deerhounds—as well as to Basenjis and Rhodesian Ridgebacks. Hounds are judged on overall ability, follow, speed, agility and endurance. This is possibly the most exciting of the trials for spectators, because the speed and agility of the dogs is awesome to watch as they chase the lure (or "course") in heats of two or three dogs at a time.

## Tracking

Tracking is another activity in which almost any dog can compete because every dog that sniffs the ground when taken outdoors is, in fact, tracking. The hard part comes when the rules as to what, when and where the dog tracks are determined by a person, not the dog! Tracking tests cover a large area of fields, woods and roads. The tracks are laid hours before the dogs go to work on them, and include "tricks" like cross-tracks and sharp turns. If you're interested in search-and-rescue work, this is the place to start.

*This tracking dog is hot on the trail.*

## Earthdog Tests for Small Terriers and Dachshunds

These tests are open to Australian, Bedlington, Border, Cairn, Dandie Dinmont, Smooth and Wire Fox, Lakeland, Norfolk, Norwich, Scottish, Sealyham, Skye, Welsh and West Highland White Terriers as well as Dachshunds. The dogs need no prior training for this terrier sport. There is a qualifying test on the day of the event, so dog and handler learn the rules on the spot. These tests, or "digs," sometimes end with informal races in the late afternoon.

133

Here are some of the extracurricular obedience and
racing activities that are not regulated by the AKC or
UKC, but are generally run by clubs or a group of dog
fanciers and are often open to all.

**Canine Freestyle** This activity is something new on
the scene and is variously likened to dancing, dressage
or ice skating. It is meant to show the athleticism of the
dog, but also requires showmanship on the part of the
dog's handler. If you and your dog like to ham it up for
friends, you might want to look into freestyle.

*Lure coursing
lets sighthounds
do what they do
best—run!*

**Scent Hurdle Racing** Scent hurdle racing is purely a
fun activity sponsored by obedience clubs with members forming competing teams. The height of the hurdles is based on the size of the shortest dog on the
team. On a signal, one team dog is released on each of
two side-by-side courses and must clear every hurdle
before picking up its own dumbbell from a platform
and returning over the jumps to the handler. As each
dog returns, the next on that team is sent. Of course,
that is what the dogs are supposed to do. When the
dogs improvise (going under or around the hurdles,
stealing another dog's dumbbell, and so forth), it no
doubt frustrates the handlers, but just adds to the fun
for everyone else.

**Flyball** This type of racing is similar, but after negoti-
ating the four hurdles, the dog comes to a flyball box,
steps on a lever that releases a tennis ball into the air,

catches the ball and returns over the hurdles to the starting point. This game also becomes extremely fun for spectators because the dogs sometimes cheat by catching a ball released by the dog in the next lane. Three titles can be earned—Flyball Dog (F.D.), Flyball Dog Excellent (F.D.X.) and Flyball Dog Champion (Fb.D.Ch.)—all awarded by the North American Flyball Association, Inc.

**Dogsledding** The name conjures up the Rocky Mountains or the frigid North, but you can find dogsled clubs in such unlikely spots as Maryland, North Carolina and Virginia! Dogsledding is primarily for the Nordic breeds such as the Alaskan Malamutes, Siberian Huskies and Samoyeds, but other breeds can try. There are some practical backyard applications to this sport, too. With parental supervision, almost any strong dog could pull a child's sled.

*Coming over the A-frame on an agility course.*

These are just some of the many recreational ways you can get to know and understand your multifaceted dog better and have fun doing it.

# chapter 10

# Your Dog
## and your
# Family

*by Bardi McLennan*

Adding a dog automatically increases your family by one, no matter whether you live alone in an apartment or are part of a mother, father and six kids household. The single-person family is fair game for numerous and varied canine misconceptions as to who is dog and who pays the bills, whereas a dog in a houseful of children will consider himself to be just one of the gang, littermates all. One dog and one child may give a dog reason to believe they are both kids or both dogs. Either interpretation requires parental supervision and sometimes speedy intervention.

As soon as one paw goes through the door into your home, Rufus (or Rufina) has to make many adjustments to become a part of your family. Your job is to make him fit in as painlessly as possible. An older dog may have some frame of reference from past experience, but to a 10-week-old puppy, everything is brand new: people, furniture, stairs, when and where people eat, sleep or watch TV, his own place and everyone else's space, smells, sounds, outdoors—everything!

Puppies, and newly acquired dogs of any age, do not need what we think of as "freedom." If you leave a new dog or puppy loose in the house, you will almost certainly return to chaotic destruction and the dog will forever after equate your homecoming with a time of punishment to be dreaded. It is unfair to give your dog what amounts to "freedom to get into trouble." Instead, confine him to a crate for brief periods of your absence (up to three or four hours) and, for the long haul, a workday for example, confine him to one untrashable area with his own toys, a bowl of water and a radio left on (low) in another room.

*Lots of pets get along with each other just fine.*

For the first few days, when not confined, put Rufus on a long leash tied to your wrist or waist. This umbilical cord method enables the dog to learn all about you from your body language and voice, and to learn by his own actions which things in the house are NO! and which ones are rewarded by "Good dog." House-training will be easier with the pup always by your side. Speaking of which, accidents do happen. That goal of "completely housetrained" takes up to a year, or the length of time it takes the pup to mature.

## The All-Adult Family

Most dogs in an adults-only household today are likely to be latchkey pets, with no one home all day but the dog. When you return after a tough day on the job, the dog can and should be your relaxation therapy. But going home can instead be a daily frustration.

Separation anxiety is a very common problem for the dog in a working household. It may begin with whines and barks of loneliness, but it will soon escalate into a frenzied destruction derby. That is why it is so important to set aside the time to teach a dog to relax when left alone in his confined area and to understand that he can trust you to return.

Let the dog get used to your work schedule in easy stages. Confine him to one room and go in and out of that room over and over again. Be casual about it. No physical, voice or eye contact. When the pup no longer even notices your comings and goings, leave the house for varying lengths of time, returning to stay home for a few minutes and gradually increasing the time away. This training can take days, but the dog is learning that you haven't left him forever and that he can trust you.

Any time you leave the dog, but especially during this training period, be casual about your departure. No anxiety-building fond farewells. Just "Bye" and go! Remember the "Good dog" when you return to find everything more or less as you left it.

If things are a mess (or even a disaster) when you return, greet the dog, take him outside to eliminate, and then put him in his crate while you clean up. Rant and rave in the shower! *Do not* punish the dog. You were not there when it happened, and the rule is: Only punish as you catch the dog in the act of wrongdoing. Obviously, it makes sense to get your latchkey puppy when you'll have a week or two to spend on these training essentials.

Family weekend activities should include Rufus whenever possible. Depending on the pup's age, now is the time for a long walk in the park, playtime in the backyard, a hike in the woods. Socializing is as important as health care, good food and physical exercise, so visiting Aunt Emma or Uncle Harry and the next-door neighbor's dog or cat is essential to developing an outgoing, friendly temperament in your pet.

If you are a single adult, socializing Rufus at home and away will prevent him from becoming overly protective of you (or just overly attached) and will also prevent such behavioral problems as dominance or fear of strangers.

# Babies

Whether already here or on the way, babies figure larger than life in the eyes of a dog. If the dog is there first, let him in on all your baby preparations in the house. When baby arrives, let Rufus sniff any item of clothing that has been on the baby before Junior comes home. Then let Mom greet the dog first before introducing the new family member. Hold the baby down for the dog to see and sniff, but make sure some-

one's holding the dog on lead in case of any sudden moves. Don't play keep-away or tease the dog with the baby, which only invites undesirable jumping up.

The dog and the baby are "family," and for starters can be treated almost as equals. Things rapidly change, however, especially when baby takes to creeping around on all fours on the dog's turf or, better yet, has yummy pudding all over her face and hands! That's when a lot of things in the dog's and baby's lives become more separate than equal.

*Dogs are perfect confidants.*

Toddlers make terrible dog owners, but if you can't avoid the combination, use patient discipline (that is, positive teaching rather than punishment), and use time-outs before you run out of patience.

A dog and a baby (or toddler, or an assertive young child) should never be left alone together. Take the dog with you or confine him. With a baby or youngsters in the house, you'll have plenty of use for that wonderful canine safety device called a crate!

# Young Children

Any dog in a house with kids will behave pretty much as the kids do, good or bad. But even good dogs and good children can get into trouble when play becomes rowdy and active.

Legs bobbing up and down, shrill voices screeching, a ball hurtling overhead, all add up to exuberant frustration for a dog who's just trying to be part of the gang. In a pack of puppies, any legs or toys being chased would be caught by a set of teeth, and all the pups involved would understand that is how the game is played. Kids do not understand this, nor do parents tolerate it. Bring Rufus indoors before you have reason to regret it. This is time-out, not a punishment.

*Teach children how to play nicely with a puppy.*

You can explain the situation to the children and tell them they must play quieter games until the puppy learns not to grab them with his mouth. Unfortunately, you can't explain it that easily to the dog. With adult supervision, they will learn how to play together.

Young children love to tease. Sticking their faces or wiggling their hands or fingers in the dog's face is teasing. To another person it might be just annoying, but it is threatening to a dog. There's another difference: We can make the child stop by an explanation, but the only way a dog can stop it is with a warning growl and then with teeth. Teasing is the major cause of children being bitten by their pets. Treat it seriously.

# Older Children

The best age for a child to get a first dog is between the ages of 8 and 12. That's when kids are able to accept some real responsibility for their pet. Even so, take the child's vow of "I will never *ever* forget to feed (brush, walk, etc.) the dog" for what it's worth: a child's good intention at that moment. Most kids today have extra lessons, soccer practice, Little League, ballet, and so forth piled on top of school schedules. There will be many times when Mom will have to come to the dog's rescue. "I walked the dog for you so you can set the table for me" is one way to get around a missed appointment without laying on blame or guilt.

Kids in this age group make excellent obedience trainers because they are into the teaching/learning process themselves and they lack the self-consciousness of adults. Attending a dog show is something the whole family can enjoy, and watching Junior Showmanship may catch the eye of the kids. Older children can begin to get involved in many of the recreational activities that were reviewed in the previous chapter. Some of the agility obstacles, for example, can be set up in the backyard as a family project (with an adult making sure all the equipment is safe and secure for the dog).

Older kids are also beginning to look to the future, and may envision themselves as veterinarians or trainers or show dog handlers or writers of the next Lassie best-seller. Dogs are perfect confidants for these dreams. They won't tell a soul.

## Other Pets

Introduce all pets tactfully. In a dog/cat situation, hold the dog, not the cat. Let two dogs meet on neutral turf—a stroll in the park or a walk down the street—with both on loose leads to permit all the normal canine ways of saying hello, including routine sniffing, circling, more sniffing, and so on. Small creatures such as hamsters, chinchillas or mice must be kept safe from their natural predators (dogs and cats).

# Festive Family Occasions

Parties are great for people, but not necessarily for puppies. Until all the guests have arrived, put the dog in his crate or in a room where he won't be disturbed. A socialized dog can join the fun later as long as he's not underfoot, annoying guests or into the hors d'oeuvres.

There are a few dangers to consider, too. Doors opening and closing can allow a puppy to slip out unnoticed in the confusion, and you'll be organizing a search party instead of playing host or hostess. Party food and buffet service are not for dogs. Let Rufus party in his crate with a nice big dog biscuit.

At Christmas time, not only are tree decorations dangerous and breakable (and perhaps family heirlooms), but extreme caution should be taken with the lights, cords and outlets for the tree lights and any other festive lighting. Occasionally a dog lifts a leg, ignoring the fact that the tree is indoors. To avoid this, use a canine repellent, made for gardens, on the tree. Or keep him out of the tree room unless supervised. And whatever you do, *don't* invite trouble by hanging his toys on the tree!

# Car Travel

Before you plan a vacation by car or RV with Rufus, be sure he enjoys car travel. Nothing spoils a holiday quicker than a carsick dog! Work within the dog's comfort level. Get in the car with the dog in his crate or attached to a canine car safety belt and just sit there until he relaxes. That's all. Next time, get in the car, turn on the engine and go nowhere. Just sit. When that is okay, turn on the engine and go around the block. Now you can go for a ride and include a stop where you get out, leaving the dog for a minute or two.

On a warm day, always park in the shade and leave windows open several inches. And return quickly. It only takes 10 minutes for a car to become an overheated steel death trap.

# Motel or Pet Motel?

Not all motels or hotels accept pets, but you have a much better choice today than even a few years ago. To find a dog-friendly lodging, look at *On the Road Again With Man's Best Friend*, a series of directories that detail bed and breakfasts, inns, family resorts and other hotels/motels. Some places require a refundable deposit to cover any damage incurred by the dog. More B&Bs accept pets now, but some restrict the size.

If taking Rufus with you is not feasible, check out boarding kennels in your area. Your veterinarian may offer this service, or recommend a kennel or two he or she is familiar with. Go see the facilities for yourself, ask about exercise, diet, housing, and so on. Or, if you'd rather have Rufus stay home, look into bonded petsitters, many of whom will also bring in the mail and water your plants.

# chapter 11

# Your Dog
## and your
# Community

*by Bardi McLennan*

Step outside your home with your dog and you are no longer just family, you are both part of your community. This is when the phrase "responsible pet ownership" takes on serious implications. For starters, it means you pick up after your dog—not just occasionally, but every time your dog eliminates away from home. That means you have joined the Plastic Baggy Brigade! You always have plastic sandwich bags in your pocket and several in the car. It means you teach your kids how to use them, too. If you think this is "yucky," just imagine what

the person (a non-doggy person) who inadvertently steps in the mess thinks!

Your responsibility extends to your neighbors: To their ears (no annoying barking); to their property (their garbage, their lawn, their flower beds, their cat—especially their cat); to their kids (on bikes, at play); to their kids' toys and sports equipment.

There are numerous dog-related laws, ranging from simple dog licensing and leash laws to those holding you liable for any physical injury or property damage done by your dog. These laws are in place to protect everyone in the community, including you and your dog. There are town ordinances and state laws which are by no means the same in all towns or all states. Ignorance of the law won't get you off the hook. The time to find out what the laws are where you live is now.

Be sure your dog's license is current. This is not just a good local ordinance, it can make the difference between finding your lost dog or not. Many states now require proof of rabies vaccination and that the dog has been spayed or neutered before issuing a license. At the same time, keep up the dog's annual immunizations.

*Dressing your dog up makes him appealing to strangers.*

Never let your dog run loose in the neighborhood. This will not only keep you on the right side of the leash law, it's the outdoor version of the rule about not giving your dog "freedom to get into trouble."

# Good Canine Citizen

Sometimes it's hard for a dog's owner to assess whether or not the dog is sufficiently socialized to be accepted by the community at large. Does Rufus or Rufina display good, controlled behavior in public? The AKC's Canine Good Citizen program is available through many dog organizations. If your dog passes the test, the title "CGC" is earned.

The overall purpose is to turn your dog into a good neighbor and to teach you about your responsibility to your community as a dog owner. Here are the ten things your dog must do willingly:

1. Accept a stranger stopping to chat with you.
2. Sit and be petted by a stranger.
3. Allow a stranger to handle him or her as a groomer or veterinarian would.
4. Walk nicely on a loose lead.
5. Walk calmly through a crowd.
6. Sit and down on command, then stay in a sit or down position while you walk away.
7. Come when called.
8. Casually greet another dog.
9. React confidently to distractions.
10. Accept being left alone with someone other than you and not become overly agitated or nervous.

## Schools and Dogs

Schools are getting involved with pet ownership on an educational level. It has been proven that children who are kind to animals are humane in their attitude toward other people as adults.

A dog is a child's best friend, and so children are often primary pet owners, if not the primary caregivers. Unfortunately, they are also the ones most often bitten by dogs. This occurs due to a lack of understanding that pets, no matter how sweet, cuddly and loving, are still animals. Schools, along with parents, dog clubs, dog fanciers and the AKC, are working to change all that with video programs for children not only in grade school, but in the nursery school and pre-kindergarten age group. Teaching youngsters how to be responsible dog owners is important community work. When your dog has a CGC, volunteer to take part in an educational classroom event put on by your dog club.

# Boy Scout Merit Badge

A Merit Badge for Dog Care can be earned by any Boy
Scout ages 11 to 18. The requirements are not easy, but
amount to a complete course in responsible dog care
and general ownership. Here are just a few of the
things a Scout must do to earn that badge:

> Point out ten parts of the dog using the correct
> names.

> Give a report (signed by parent or guardian) on
> your care of the dog (feeding, food used, housing,
> exercising, grooming and bathing), plus what has
> been done to keep the dog healthy.

> Explain the right way to obedience train a dog,
> and demonstrate three comments.

> Several of the requirements have to do with health
> care, including first aid, handling a hurt dog, and
> the dangers of home treatment for a serious
> ailment.

> The final requirement is to know the local laws
> and ordinances involving dogs.

There are similar programs for Girl Scouts and 4-H
members.

# Local Clubs

Local dog clubs are no longer in existence just to put
on a yearly dog show. Today, they are apt to be the hub
of the community's involvement with pets. Dog clubs
conduct educational forums with big-name speakers,
stage demonstrations of canine talent in a busy mall
and take dogs of various breeds to schools for classroom discussion.

The quickest way to feel accepted as a member in a
club is to volunteer your services! Offer to help with
something—anything—and watch your popularity
(and your interest) grow.

# Therapy Dogs

Once your dog has earned that essential CGC and reliably demonstrates a steady, calm temperament, you could look into what therapy dogs are doing in your area.

Therapy dogs go with their owners to visit patients at hospitals or nursing homes, generally remaining on leash but able to coax a pat from a stiffened hand, a smile from a blank face, a few words from sealed lips or a hug from someone in need of love.

Nursing homes cover a wide range of patient care. Some specialize in care of the elderly, some in the treatment of specific illnesses, some in physical therapy. Children's facilities also welcome visits from trained therapy dogs for boosting morale in their pediatric patients. Hospice care for the terminally ill and the at-home care of AIDS patients are other areas where this canine visiting is desperately needed. Therapy dog training comes first.

*Your dog can make a difference in lots of lives.*

There is a lot more involved than just taking your nice friendly pooch to someone's bedside. Doing therapy dog work involves your own emotional stability as well as that of your dog. But once you have met all the requirements for this work, making the rounds once a week or once a month with your therapy dog is possibly the most rewarding of all community activities.

# Disaster Aid

This community service is definitely not for everyone, partly because it is time-consuming. The initial training is rigorous, and there can be no let-up in the continuing workouts, because members are on call 24 hours a day to go wherever they are needed at a moment's notice. But if you think you would like to be able to assist in a disaster, look into search-and-rescue work. The network of search-and-rescue volunteers is worldwide, and all members of the American Rescue Dog Association (ARDA) who are qualified to do this work are volunteers who train and maintain their own dogs.

## Physical Aid

Most people are familiar with Seeing Eye dogs, which serve as blind people's eyes, but not with all the other work that dogs are trained to do to assist the disabled. Dogs are also specially trained to pull wheelchairs, carry school books, pick up dropped objects, open and close doors. Some also are ears for the deaf. All these assistance-trained dogs, by the way, are allowed anywhere "No Pet" signs exist (as are therapy dogs when

*Making the rounds with your therapy dog can be very rewarding.*

properly identified). Getting started in any of this fascinating work requires a background in dog training and canine behavior, but there are also volunteer jobs ranging from answering the phone to cleaning out kennels to providing a foster home for a puppy. You have only to ask.

# part four

Beyond the Basics

# chapter 12

# Recommended Reading

## Books

### ABOUT HEALTH CARE

Ackerman, Lowell. *Guide to Skin and Haircoat Problems in Dogs*. Loveland, Colo.: Alpine Publications, 1994.

Alderton, David. *The Dog Care Manual*. Hauppauge, N.Y.: Barron's Educational Series, Inc., 1986.

American Kennel Club. *American Kennel Club Dog Care and Training*. New York: Howell Book House, 1991.

Bamberger, Michelle, DVM. *Help! The Quick Guide to First Aid for Your Dog*. New York: Howell Book House, 1995.

Carlson, Delbert, DVM, and James Giffin, MD. *Dog Owner's Home Veterinary Handbook*. New York: Howell Book House, 1992.

DeBitetto, James, DVM, and Sarah Hodgson. *You & Your Puppy*. New York: Howell Book House, 1995.

Humphries, Jim, DVM. *Dr. Jim's Animal Clinic for Dogs*. New York: Howell Book House, 1994.

McGinnis, Terri. *The Well Dog Book*. New York: Random House, 1991.

Pitcairn, Richard and Susan. *Natural Health for Dogs*. Emmaus, Pa.: Rodale Press, 1982.

### ABOUT DOG SHOWS

Hall, Lynn. *Dog Showing for Beginners*. New York: Howell Book House, 1994.

Nichols, Virginia Tuck. *How to Show Your Own Dog*. Neptune, N. J.: TFH, 1970.

Vanacore, Connie. *Dog Showing, An Owner's Guide*. New York: Howell Book House, 1990.

## ABOUT TRAINING

Ammen, Amy. *Training in No Time.* New York: Howell Book House, 1995.

Baer, Ted. *Communicating With Your Dog.* Hauppauge, N.Y.: Barron's Educational Series, Inc., 1989.

Benjamin, Carol Lea. *Dog Problems.* New York: Howell Book House, 1989.

Benjamin, Carol Lea. *Dog Training for Kids.* New York: Howell Book House, 1988.

Benjamin, Carol Lea. *Mother Knows Best.* New York: Howell Book House, 1985.

Benjamin, Carol Lea. *Surviving Your Dog's Adolescence.* New York: Howell Book House, 1993.

Bohnenkamp, Gwen. *Manners for the Modern Dog.* San Francisco: Perfect Paws, 1990.

Dibra, Bashkim. *Dog Training by Bash.* New York: Dell, 1992.

Dunbar, Ian, PhD, MRCVS. *Dr. Dunbar's Good Little Dog Book,* James & Kenneth Publishers, 2140 Shattuck Ave. #2406, Berkeley, Calif. 94704. (510) 658–8588. Order from the publisher.

Dunbar, Ian, PhD, MRCVS. *How to Teach a New Dog Old Tricks,* James & Kenneth Publishers. Order from the publisher; address above.

Dunbar, Ian, PhD, MRCVS, and Gwen Bohnenkamp. Booklets on *Preventing Aggression; Housetraining; Chewing; Digging; Barking; Socialization; Fearfulness; and Fighting,* James & Kenneth Publishers. Order from the publisher; address above.

Evans, Job Michael. *People, Pooches and Problems.* New York: Howell Book House, 1991.

Kilcommons, Brian and Sarah Wilson. *Good Owners, Great Dogs.* New York: Warner Books, 1992.

McMains, Joel M. *Dog Logic—Companion Obedience.* New York: Howell Book House, 1992.

Rutherford, Clarice and David H. Neil, MRCVS. *How to Raise a Puppy You Can Live With.* Loveland, Colo.: Alpine Publications, 1982.

Volhard, Jack and Melissa Bartlett. *What All Good Dogs Should Know: The Sensible Way to Train.* New York: Howell Book House, 1991.

## ABOUT BREEDING

Harris, Beth J. Finder. *Breeding a Litter, The Complete Book of Prenatal and Postnatal Care.* New York: Howell Book House, 1983.

Holst, Phyllis, DVM. *Canine Reproduction.* Loveland, Colo.: Alpine Publications, 1985.

Walkowicz, Chris and Bonnie Wilcox, DVM. *Successful Dog Breeding, The Complete Handbook of Canine Midwifery.* New York: Howell Book House, 1994.

## ABOUT ACTIVITIES

American Rescue Dog Association. *Search and Rescue Dogs.* New York: Howell Book House, 1991.

Barwig, Susan and Stewart Hilliard. *Schutzhund.* New York: Howell Book House, 1991.

Beaman, Arthur S. *Lure Coursing.* New York: Howell Book House, 1994.

Daniels, Julie. *Enjoying Dog Agility—From Backyard to Competition.* New York: Doral Publishing, 1990.

Davis, Kathy Diamond. *Therapy Dogs.* New York: Howell Book House, 1992.

Gallup, Davis Anne. *Running With Man's Best Friend.* Loveland, Colo.: Alpine Publications, 1986.

Habgood, Dawn and Robert. *On the Road Again With Man's Best Friend.* New England, Mid-Atlantic, West Coast and Southeast editions. Selective guides to area bed and breakfasts, inns, hotels and resorts that welcome guests and their dogs. New York: Howell Book House, 1995.

Holland, Vergil S. *Herding Dogs.* New York: Howell Book House, 1994.

LaBelle, Charlene G. *Backpacking With Your Dog.* Loveland, Colo.: Alpine Publications, 1993.

Simmons-Moake, Jane. *Agility Training, The Fun Sport for All Dogs.* New York: Howell Book House, 1991.

Spencer, James B. *Hup! Training Flushing Spaniels the American Way.* New York: Howell Book House, 1992.

Spencer, James B. *Point! Training the All-Seasons Birddog.* New York: Howell Book House, 1995.

Tarrant, Bill. *Training the Hunting Retriever.* New York: Howell Book House, 1991.

Volhard, Jack and Wendy. *The Canine Good Citizen.* New York: Howell Book House, 1994.

# General Titles

Haggerty, Captain Arthur J. *How to Get Your Pet Into Show Business.* New York: Howell Book House, 1994.

McLennan, Bardi. *Dogs and Kids, Parenting Tips.* New York: Howell Book House, 1993.

Moran, Patti J. *Pet Sitting for Profit, A Complete Manual for Professional Success.* New York: Howell Book House, 1992.

Scalisi, Danny and Libby Moses. *When Rover Just Won't Do, Over 2,000 Suggestions for Naming Your Dog.* New York: Howell Book House, 1993.

Sife, Wallace, PhD. *The Loss of a Pet.* New York: Howell Book House, 1993.

Wrede, Barbara J. *Civilizing Your Puppy.* Hauppauge, N.Y.: Barron's Educational Series, 1992.

# Magazines

*The AKC GAZETTE, The Official Journal for the Sport of Purebred Dogs.* American Kennel Club, 51 Madison Ave., New York, NY.

*Bloodlines Journal.* United Kennel Club, 100 E. Kilgore Rd., Kalamazoo, MI.

*Dog Fancy.* Fancy Publications, 3 Burroughs, Irvine, CA 92718

*Dog World.* Maclean Hunter Publishing Corp., 29 N. Wacker Dr., Chicago, IL 60606.

# Videos

"SIRIUS Puppy Training," by Ian Dunbar, PhD, MRCVS. James & Kenneth Publishers, 2140 Shattuck Ave. #2406, Berkeley, CA 94704. Order from the publisher.

"Training the Companion Dog," from Dr. Dunbar's British TV Series, James & Kenneth Publishers. (See address above).

The American Kennel Club produces videos on every breed of dog, as well as on hunting tests, field trials and other areas of interest to purebred dog owners. For more information, write to AKC/Video Fulfillment, 5580 Centerview Dr., Suite 200, Raleigh, NC 27606.

# Resources

## Breed Clubs

Every breed recognized by the American Kennel Club has a national (parent) club. National clubs are a great source of information on your breed. You can get the name of the secretary of the club by contacting:

**The American Kennel Club**
51 Madison Avenue
New York, NY 10010
(212) 696-8200

There are also numerous all-breed, individual breed, obedience, hunting and other special-interest dog clubs across the country. The American Kennel Club can provide you with a geographical list of clubs to find ones in your area. Contact them at the above address.

## Registry Organizations

Registry organizations register purebred dogs. The American Kennel Club is the oldest and largest in this country, and currently recognizes over 130 breeds. The United Kennel Club registers some breeds the AKC doesn't (including the American Pit Bull Terrier and the Miniature Fox Terrier) as well as many of the same breeds. The others included here are for your reference; the AKC can provide you with a list of foreign registries.

**American Kennel Club**
51 Madison Avenue
New York, NY 10010

**United Kennel Club (UKC)**
100 E. Kilgore Road
Kalamazoo, MI 49001-5598

**American Dog Breeders Assn.**
P.O. Box 1771
Salt Lake City, UT 84110
(Registers American Pit Bull Terriers)

**Canadian Kennel Club**
89 Skyway Avenue
Etobicoke, Ontario
Canada M9W 6R4

**National Stock Dog Registry**
P.O. Box 402
Butler, IN 46721
(Registers working stock dogs)

**Orthopedic Foundation for Animals (OFA)**
2300 E. Nifong Blvd.
Columbia, MO 65201-3856
(Hip registry)

## Activity Clubs

Write to these organizations for information on the activities they sponsor.

**American Kennel Club**
51 Madison Avenue
New York, NY 10010
(Conformation Shows, Obedience Trials, Field
Trials and Hunting Tests, Agility, Canine Good

Citizen, Lure Coursing, Herding, Tracking, Earthdog Tests, Coonhunting.)

**United Kennel Club**
100 E. Kilgore Road
Kalamazoo, MI 49001-5598
(Conformation Shows, Obedience Trials, Agility, Hunting for Various Breeds, Terrier Trials and more.)

**North American Flyball Assn.**
1342 Jeff St.
Ypsilanti, MI 48198

**International Sled Dog Racing Assn.**
P.O. Box 446
Norman, ID 83848-0446

**North American Working Dog Assn., Inc.**
Southeast Kreisgruppe
P.O. Box 833
Brunswick, GA 31521

# Trainers

**Association of Pet Dog Trainers**
P.O. Box 385
Davis, CA 95617
(800) PET–DOGS

**American Dog Trainers' Network**
161 West 4th St.
New York, NY 10014
(212) 727–7257

**National Association of Dog Obedience Instructors**
2286 East Steel Rd.
St. Johns, MI 48879

# Associations

**American Dog Owners Assn.**
1654 Columbia Tpk.
Castleton, NY 12033
(Combats anti-dog legislation)

**Delta Society**
P.O. Box 1080
Renton, WA 98057-1080
(Promotes the human/animal bond through
pet-assisted therapy and other programs)

**Dog Writers Assn. of America (DWAA)**
Sally Cooper, Secy.
222 Woodchuck Ln.
Harwinton, CT 06791

**National Assn. for Search and Rescue (NASAR)**
P.O. Box 3709
Fairfax, VA 22038

**Therapy Dogs International**
6 Hilltop Road
Mendham, NJ 07945